REGAL REALM

REGAL REALM

A WORLD CHAMPION'S STORY

LUCINDA GREEN MBE

PELHAM BOOKS
LONDON

First published in Great Britain by
Pelham Books Ltd
44 Bedford Square
London WC1B 3DU
1983

British Library Cataloguing in Publication Data

Green, Lucinda
Regal Realm
1. Regal Realm (Horse)
I. Title
798.2'4   SF295.5

ISBN 0 7207 1471 0

Filmset by Northumberland Press Ltd, Gateshead
Printed and bound in Great Britain by
Richard Clay (The Chaucer Press) Ltd, Bungay, Suffolk

FRONTISPIECE: Lucinda Green and Regal Realm. (*Stuart Newsham*)

To HB with all my love. LM

By the same author

UP, UP AND AWAY
The Biography of Be Fair

FOUR SQUARE
A Tribute to Be Fair, Wide Awake, George and Killaire

CONTENTS

Preface
9

Acknowledgments
11

Introduction
Explanation of a Three-Day Event
13

REGAL REALM
15

Epilogue
178

Appendix 1
World Championship Results
179

Appendix 2
Interval Training
182

Appendix 3
Vital Statistics
185

PREFACE

Why should horses race? Why should they jump? Why should they be pawns to man's whims?

These questions are occasionally asked. Before the following story with its inevitable ups and downs is read, I would like to offer my response to those who may query.

I believe that children, horses and dogs alike need a framework of discipline within which to weave an auspicious life. It is this framework itself and not the lack of it which produces happiness and liberty. Most certainly there are in this world some disreputable framemakers – but that is life. Despite those imperfections I would prefer to see children, horses and dogs taught a code of discipline as opposed to being left to fend for themselves.

Have you met any of those odious children who have been brought up in a specific manner, in which there lies no parental ruling or criticism? Have you seen Battersea Dogs' Home at Christmas, or New Forest ponies, gaunt and sad as they search for a scrap of food in the middle of winter?

Have you, on the other hand, seen Killaire's face radiating fulfilment as he headed the line-up at Badminton, or Village Gossip's as he delights in his own ability to gallop and jump? You never did see the forlorn and miserable figure that was Be Fair as he sloped around the field in his retirement watching the horse-box chug daily down the drive without him.

Many thousands of horses are cared for lavishly. If there were not such an abundance of professions in which the horse could be employed, the ratio of well-kept animals to neglected ones could well be reversed.

ACKNOWLEDGMENTS

To Sir Alec Creswick for breeding Regal Realm and his aid in my investigations into this horse's earliest days.

To Mervyn, Ann and Jodie Bennett for all their help in telling me of Regal Realm's past.

To Nancy Green, my mother-in-law, who typed the entire manuscript from an appalling mess of words, thereby making it possible to produce the book in time for publication in 1983.

To *Riding* magazine for allowing me to use photographs and excerpts from articles I have written for them over the last four years.

To Stuart Newsham and his wife, for their tremendous help in taking so many excellent photographs in great haste to keep the printer's deadline.

To Caroline Silver, Michael Sissons and Eric Marriott, without whose early encouragement I would never have begun to try and write.

To my mother, whose wisdom and courage I will admire forever.

To my brother Simon, without whose patience and business brain I would have been lost many times.

To all the sponsors who make it possible for our sport and its participants to continue.

To all those kind and hard-working people who rarely receive personal acknowledgment but without whom there would be no competitions and no story to tell. The British Equestrian Federation, the British Horse Society, landowners, fence judges, coursebuilders, car-park attendants, St John Ambulance and Red Cross, arena parties, scorers, secretaries and organisers, are but a few of those to whom I would like to extend my warmest thanks.

Finally a special acknowledgment to Lesley Gowers of Pelham Books who has edited all three of my books and without whose support and kind, light-hearted attitude the first one would never have seen a bookshelf, let alone the following two.

INTRODUCTION

Explanation of a Three-day Event

Three-day eventing is a sport which originated as a military test of speed and stamina required in a horse and rider who were to carry important messages over long distances.

On the first day the dressage test is performed. This was conceived to ensure that a very fit horse was sufficiently disciplined to be able to perform a controlled series of prescribed movements in a small area.

The middle day – the speed and endurance test – was, and still is, the crux of the competition. In modern-day eventing this test is split into four phases. Phases A and C are approximately 3 and 7 miles in length respectively. They consist of specified routes along roads and tracks and across fields of all types of terrain. The pace at which these two phases are negotiated is either a fairly consistent trot, or a canter and walk.

Dividing these two phases is the steeplechase – Phase B. This varies in length from 1½ to 2 miles and includes between eight and ten obstacles with a maximum height of 4 ft 6 ins. The speed is a gallop.

A compulsory ten-minute break follows Phase C. Here the horse's state of health and fitness is checked by a vet and a panel forming the ground jury. They have the right to force the retirement of any horse they feel is not fit to continue. During this break the horse may be dismounted and washed down if required.

The all-important cross-country phase – Phase D – completes the test on that day. The course ranges from between 4 and 5 miles in length with twenty-five to thirty-five numbered obstacles. The optimum speed at which this must be tackled is mid-way between a slow canter and a steeplechase gallop.

If, in any of the four phases, the competitor is found to be outside the time allowed, penalty points will be awarded and these

13

will be added to whatever penalties have been accumulated at obstacles: 20 for a refusal or run-out within the penalty-zone of a fence (this zone is a rectangular area drawn 10 yards in front and to the sides of the fence and 20 yards beyond it); 60 penalties for a fall within the penalty zone.

The maximum permitted height and spread of a cross-country fence, 3 ft 11 ins by 6 ft 6 ins, does not make a very big fence, but when built of massive ungiving timber, roped to the trunks of trees, such an obstacle can look very imposing. Possibly the most testing fence on a course will be only 2 ft 9 ins high, for the degree of difficulty may depend entirely on the gradient of the take-off or landing, or on what may lurk before or behind it.

At the end of cross-country day, when the penalties have been added to those received during the previous day's dressage, the leader is the one with the lowest score.

On the third day, after the second official vets' inspection (the first vetting takes place before the competition begins) the final phase, the show-jumping, is held. The course is not big – it measures no more than 3 ft 11 ins in height – but it is a test designed to demonstrate that the horse is still supple and obedient and able to jump well after the previous day. If a horse has been pushed too hard on cross-country day, more than likely he will be too tired to show-jump properly twenty-four hours later.

There are no penalty zones on the show-jumping course. A fall anywhere in the arena carries 30 penalties, a refusal 10 penalties, and a knock-down 5 penalties.

Many great performances have been witnessed in the cross-country phase, where the combined confidence of a horse and rider has produced courage and skill that has superseded the toughest of courses. However, the final result hangs in the balance until the show-jumping is completed. Many a personal triumph has been transformed into an historically unremarkable achievement through the tipping of just one of those ten or twelve coloured fences.

1

In 1971 Be Fair gave me my earliest memorable moment. He was a member of the three-day event team that credited Britain with her first gold medal in the Junior European Championships.

On the other side of the world a brown mare, typical of the small station-bred thoroughbred of northern New South Wales, gave birth to a colt foal. Between his big black eyes was a white star which gave into a thin blaze running three parts of the way down his face. He also owned Be Fair's 'lucky white sock' on his near hind leg. He was just one of thirty foals who, together with their mothers, roamed a vast two-thousand acre paddock. The fenced boundary line lay beyond the horizon and out of sight on the eighty-six square mile property of Comboglong near Coonamble. The stallion Taunton, distantly related to a racehorse that had been placed third in the Melbourne Cup, ran all the year round with these mares.

Occasionally, mounted stockmen would ride through the group to check them. Apart from these men the foals saw nothing other than endless flat stretches of land covered by wispy brownish grass. Only a few spindly trees offered shelter from the fierce summer sun and temperatures of over 100°F. The horses inhabited the silence that dominates the Australian outback, their peace undisturbed.

Later in the year, about nine months after the foals had been born, some station hands, wearing broad-brimmed felt hats and each equipped with a long plaited-leather stock-whip, rode along-side them. The colt with the appealing black eyes hopped and sprang back to his mother.

With dust kicking up all about them, the mares and their off-spring were herded several miles back to the homestead. There they were driven into a sorting yard whose six-foot high railings

Part of a herd of mares grazing in a sparse 2,000-acre paddock near Comboglong in northern New South Wales. All around them barren land, covered by wispy brownish grass, stretches into the distance. (*David Green*)

offered no escape. One at a time the foals were channelled into a narrow chute. The unknown smell of the branding-iron was enough to warn the youngster that he was in some sort of danger, but what sort he could not know. Before he had time to think, a rope was slung around his neck, his legs were hobbled together and he was thrown onto his off-side. A hot iron was planted firmly on his near-side quarter imprinting the figures '71', indicating the year of his birth. On his near shoulder was burnt the station brand – a triangle – and the thoroughbred stud book number.

This was the first time in his life that he had been touched by man, and it was only the start of the frightening day that station-bred youngstock have to endure.

Next a long tube was slipped down the colt's throat and into his stomach. Several pints of liquid wormer were poured down

16

the tube. Following that, strong men held the foal on his side, clamped against the railings, as another took a sharpened knife and gelded him.

When the bleeding from this barbaric but necessary operation eventually ceased, all the youngsters were turned out into another vast paddock – but this time they were alone. Gone was their father figure, the striking bay Taunton; and no longer was there a mother to nestle up to in times of fear or distress.

For the next year and a half the youngsters barely saw any human beings. Without the shadow of their mothers they roamed further afield in their enormous featureless territory. They drank at the edge of a man-made hollow, a dam. They ate what shrubbery they could find to complement their basic diet of coarse, yellowy Mitchell grass. In the winter the grass grew to three feet in height but in the summer drought there was little to be found.

It was in the summertime, when the food was at its starkest, the sun at its angriest and the youngsters at their leanest and most biddable that the station hands came once again, cracking their whips. It was time for these two-year-olds to learn to earn their keep.

Once again they were rounded up into the sorting yard. There they waited, fending off the worst of the flies as they roasted in the sun. One by one the skinny young horses were let into a smaller round enclosure where they could be caught more easily and eventually succumb to having a halter placed on their heads.

Poncho, as they came to name the one with the white star and blaze, was nervous and not an easy proposition to tame. He did not trust. He was highly strung and very quick witted. The last time he had been in close contact with men, eighteen months earlier, they had hurt him. He had no intention of letting this happen again.

After a while he relented in so far as he would allow the men to bridle him. Then, as he stood uneasily, anticipating their next move, he saw one of them holding up a piece of blanket. Poncho jumped and fidgetted every time this strange piece of material came near him. He swung his tense body from side to side in an effort to avoid the blanket's touch.

With still another dozen animals left to deal with that morning, the stockmen did not have time to waste. They had met Poncho's

17

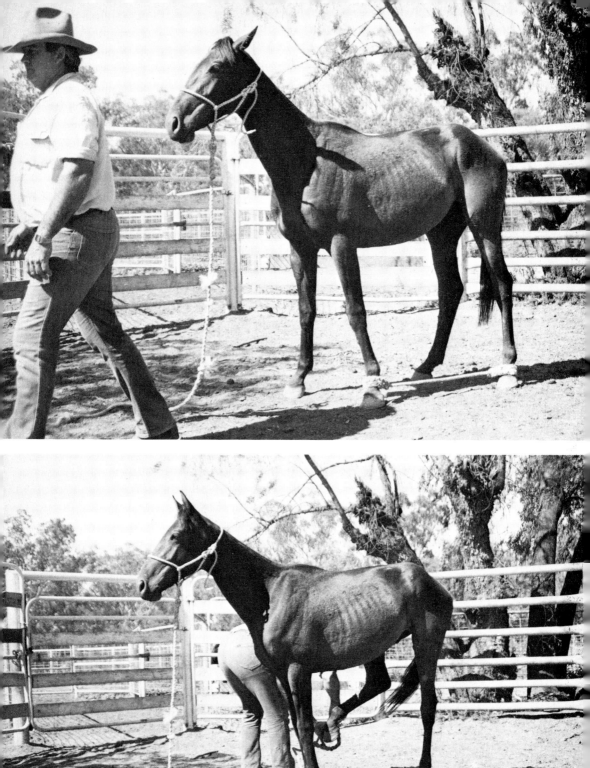

type before. They knew what do do. Quietly bending down they encouraged Poncho to lift his near front foot. When he did so they looped a leather collar over his foot onto his pastern. Attached to this collar were twenty-eight inches of rope with a similar leather loop at the other end. After a little persuasion and some jagged kicks from the two-year-old the near-hind foot was lifted forwards and the second collar quickly slipped on. The process was repeated on the off side. As Poncho went to move a pace, he felt the leather loops tighten around his pasterns. He kicked out violently with his near-hind and in so doing pulled his near-foreleg back underneath him, nearly falling onto his shoulder. Scrambling to regain his balance he began to thrash around and leap into the air. He had to rid himself of this restriction, regain his freedom. The more he fought the more unbalanced he became. In less than a minute he had given himself a fall. The dust hung in the air as he struggled to his feet and stood there, his wide baby eyes staring, his body trembling, the sweat from his exertions beginning to darken his neck.

The men approached him. He did not move, he dared not. Quietly one man held him and another began to rub his back and sides with the piece of blanket.

Each evening the youngstock were herded out of the yard and loosed into a large paddock near the homestead. In the morning they were rounded up and returned to the yard. Each day after they had caught him, the men put Poncho's feet in side-lines, as these restraints are known, before they did anything else with him.

He made a second attempt to free himself of his side-lines when the heavy stock saddle was girthed up for the first time. However, he soon realised he had no option and stopped still before he fell over.

Side-lines are a fascinating invention from the Australian Bush. They are simple yet effective, for the horse is merely fighting himself. It is a scaring procedure to witness because when the horse does lose his balance he can crash down very heavily. It is like

---

Attaching side-lines to a two-year-old stock horse before he is saddled for the first time. The condition of this youngster is typical of such horses in the droughts of summer. (*David Green*)

19

ABOVE: An Australian stock saddle. The upper thigh pad and deep, well-stuffed seat enable a stockman to ride all day without becoming too saddle weary. Note also the thick saddle blankets necessary to protect the sharp withers of a skinny young horse from rubbing against the heavy saddle. (*David Green*)

OPPOSITE ABOVE: With side-lines attached and saddle secured, the two-year-old is mounted. The long, unjoined reins are used both as a whip and to tether the horse. (*David Green*)

OPPOSITE BELOW: Side-lines released, the youngster is persuaded forwards. (*David Green*)

a person falling over and being unable to put an arm out to lessen the blow.

Poncho had soon accepted the bridle, the saddle and the weight of a man. Next he had to learn to go forwards when asked. Without fuss the side-lines were released. At first Poncho did not realise his freedom, but gradually as he walked and jogged about the small, round yard, he began to notice his legs were no longer tied together.

He roached his back and sprang into the air, all four feet at once. His head was planted on his chest, his legs ramrod straight. Like a pogo-stick he plunged his way around the small area in a series of staccato bounds, twisting this way and that. He had little shoulder or neck and was extremely narrow to sit on. He moved at the speed of light from side to side. He was not an easy horse to break in.

By the end of their first week of civilisation all thirty young horses were broken and ridden. All their manes had been hogged, as they inhabited a country full of burrs. With a 55,000-acre cattle station to cover, each jackaroo (or stockman) needed several horses, especially as the two-year-olds were not strong enough to do more than a few hours' work each day.

At some time during his early months of working the cattle, the little razor-blade of a stock horse made another serious endeavour to discharge himself of his burden. It might have been then that his rider pulled Poncho's head up from his chest when he began to curl up and buck. In so doing the low-slung bit could have caught on the bottom off-side eye tooth and ripped it by the roots until it lay horizontally along the bar of his mouth. From such an injury he would have suffered much pain, and the memory of this incident was probably the reason why he carried his head so high and was so reluctant ever to lower it again.

As he grew and developed, so his jaw-bone became malformed in the area where the tooth root had been torn. The hole calloused over and was not discovered for another seven years.

Gradually Poncho must have deemed it prudent to allow the head-strong desires of his youth to give way to the genuine trier that is his foundation.

Soon he became the one stock horse on the property that all the jackaroos wanted to ride. He was brilliant with the cattle.

Quick, nimble and incredibly surefooted, he would follow and head off a straying calf or a head of cattle wherever it went. Many of the friends he had been brought up with were either sold to similar properties or used for other purposes. If they were good for nothing they were culled. Poncho found himself working longer and longer days, so able was he at his job.

Despite his talents he would not be shod. The smell of the fire, the clanging of the heavy tools reminded him all too clearly of that dreadful day when, at only nine months old, his peaceful existence was interrupted so abruptly. Instead, his feet grew broad and flat, somewhat resembling a camel's. They pounded against the iron ground, sometimes for ten hours a day, seven days a week.

The 1976 Montreal Games were surrounded by a tightly woven mesh of security. Only four years earlier eleven Israeli athletes had been murdered in the Munich Olympic village. The Canadians' responsibility for the athletes' safety in Montreal was correspondingly massive.

For this reason each participant, trainer, attendant and relative had to wear an identity photo on a special card, hung around his or her neck.

Shortly after the Australian three-day event team arrived in Bromont, they struck trouble. Their *chef d'équipe*, Sir Alec Creswick, and several of his riders, including Mervyn Bennett, were held up in their mini-bus at a road block.

All, save for Sir Alec, descended and showed their identity cards. 'And that ... who is that in there?' questioned a security guard, pointing at Sir Alec.

'Creswick, Sir Alec, a Knight of the Realm,' replied Sir Alec with dignity.

'Out, everybody I said. Out. Everybody out!' ordered an infuriated guard.

On many occasions such a magnificent proclamation would have produced the desired results. This time, however, Sir Alec had stumbled on a French Canadian, a race not known to favour the Monarchy.

Merv Bennett finished twelfth in the Olympic Games on Regal Reign, a six-year-old horse that had completed only one preparatory three-day event. During that time Merv and his wife Ann first became acquainted with Sir Alec.

At Montreal my first horse, Be Fair, who had taken me at fifteen years old through Pony Club and eventually on to the Olympic Games, saw his seven-year fairy-tale career brought to an abrupt close. He slipped the Achilles tendon off his hock as he turned to gallop for the finish of the cross-country phase after a medal-winning round. Sir Alec, having commiserated with my father, then reminded him of half a century earlier. In 1926, his own father, Harry Creswick, had lent a string of polo ponies to the team representing the British Army in India that came to play in Australia. My father was a member; he was twenty-three years old, exactly my age at the time of Montreal.

Merv Bennett. (*Findlay Davidson*)

Since the early fifties Sir Alec had supplied Bill Roycroft and other famous Australian three-day eventers with many of their horses for the Olympic Games. He had one particularly good blood-line from a mare whose mother was a big winner on the racecourse and by a sire called Sentaway, the father of Taunton and of a number of Olympic horses during the past twenty years.

Bill Roycroft's fifth and final Olympics was Montreal where he competed on a lovely tough type of horse called Version. Sir Alec believed that Merv Bennett would probably take Bill's place as the mainstay of the Australian team for another decade or two. Therefore when Merv telephoned him after Montreal to discover whether or not he knew of any young, potentially top-class horses that could be bought and aimed towards Moscow, the answer was affirmative.

Although he lived in Victoria, Sir Alec's horse breeding took place on his property near Coonamble in northern New South Wales. From blood-lines alone he knew he had a gelding out there who was rising six and should fit Merv's requirements. Version was the most recently celebrated relation of this young horse who for three years had known only the long rough day that is the life of the Australian stock horse.

Shortly before Christmas in 1976 Sir Alec and Merv went north to Comboglong station, Coonamble.

Sir Alec picked out a small, wiry creature whose coat was bleached nearly yellow by the sun. His name was Poncho. He assured Merv that there were no strings attached; he could have the horse and if he was no good he could sell him on. All Sir Alec requested was that Poncho should be entered in the combined ownership of himself and the Bennetts.

This was not the horse Merv had expected, nor really the horse he wanted. He is a tall stringy man, who does not weigh much but, in his own words, he rides heavy. Poncho could possibly measure 16 hands in height, but he resembled little more than a pony in every other respect.

For over twenty years Sir Alec Creswick had been picking out, as youngsters, horses of potential Olympic calibre. He must know. Merv accepted his generous offer, agreeing with Sir Alec not to drive up to collect the horse for another four weeks as Poncho would need a month's 'spell' (holiday) to put on enough condition to withstand the long, hot journey south.

Early in the New Year of 1977, Merv and Ann made the expedition to Coonamble in their truck. January is the hottest time of the year in Australia and they both hoped Poncho would be strong enough to cope with the rigours of a 550-mile journey.

His condition had not altered. They found him in a stable, with sweat marks on his back, indicating that a saddle had been off him barely an hour. There were raw patches on either side of his withers where the heavy stock saddle had rubbed. An ugly scar was still suppurating half way down his neck. He had apparently been savaged by another horse during night time, when all the stock horses roamed a paddock together.

An inquiry was made as to why this horse had not been 'spelled' as instructed by the boss a month ago. The stockmen answered angrily that Poncho was too good to spell, 'He's even used to fetch in the house-cow.' As long as the little whippet remained on the

The ugly scar left on Poncho's neck after he had been savaged by another horse. (*David Green*)

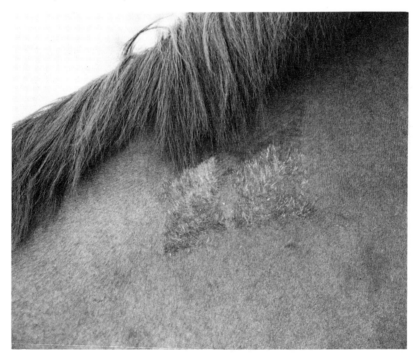

station it was clear that he was having no holiday.

The Bennetts decided to give Poncho a break in the journey. About half way the truck stopped at a 'pub' (an Australian inn) and Poncho was loosed into a tiny paddock at the rear. Later in the evening, before the sun sank and allowed in the welcome cool, several of the clientele came out from the pub to view this new horse. They knew that Merv had not long returned from the Olympic Games and they all wanted to see his future candidate.

Tired by his journey, tired by his life, the skinny, diminutive yellowed creature, with his staring, slightly fluffy coat, mostly turning back the wrong way, stood picking at bare stalks. He looked up for a moment as the strangers approached his paddock. No excitement showed on their faces and no excitement or interest showed on his.

Poncho's new home was in Nowra, southern New South Wales. For the first two months nothing much was done with him. Once his saddle sores had healed, leaving white hairs growing in their place, he was hacked around the Bennetts' property by Ann and thirteen-year-old daughter, Jodie. Once he began to gain some strength Merv and Ann set about the long task of trying to teach him to accept the bit. He had the lightest mouth but carried his head high, on the end of an upside-down neck, and always held himself off the bit. Like any good cattle horse the reins only had to be picked up and he would stop. Therefore every time a contact was given, however delicate, he would back away from it and any forward impulsion he had would be lost. He could never forget the pain he once felt when he leaned down on the bit to buck. With great patience the pair spent many hours over the next three years trying to dare him to stretch himself onto the bit. The slightest movement from the rider or a request for a transition from one pace to another, and the little horse whacked his ears back and drew his head up horizontal to the ground as he ewed and concertina'ed his neck. Similarly, so acutely sensitive was he that if he felt his rider's weight shift slightly sideways, he would turn that way immediately.

At times, early on, when he did bring his head down he began to buck. After suffering this for a while, Merv deemed it wise to let him have his head up for a bit longer and concentrate on some jumping training instead.

Poncho, two months after he left the cattle station. (*Ann Bennett*)

He was still unsure whether to keep Poncho or the beautifully moving 16.2 hh five-year-old he had bought off the racetrack the year before. He rode them both down a jumping lane, where the oddly spaced obstacles were no more than eighteen inches high. The fluid, long strides of the ex-racehorse landed him in all sorts of trouble. Although it was the first time Poncho saw a jump, let alone a line of them, with his clever little strides, never cut out for the elegance of dressage, he found the grid no problem.

Merv always picked his horses on their jumping ability. Despite knowing he was somewhat underhorsed, he felt there was no fence too big for this little stock horse. The graceful racehorse was therefore the one who was moved out.

Poncho knew nothing of the world outside the stretches of a flat, sparsely wooded plain with its cattle dogs and kangaroos. When Merv first rode Poncho, he could not prevent him from diving into the undergrowth in fast pursuit of his Labradors; Poncho was so highly self-trained that he would not take his eyes off the dogs, which he presumed were straying calves. Traffic was an unknown phenomenon and so was shoeing. As both made a great deal of noise he was not keen to become acquainted with either.

Merv first knew what sort of temperament his young horse had when he decided that, at six years old, it was time he was shod. He threw his tools down beside the tethered horse and instantly Poncho pulled away and began to blow a snorting whistle down his nostrils. His neck arched as he continued to snort in horror at what lay on the floor in front of him. Eventually he calmed down enough for Merv to begin his job. Such was Poncho's mistrust of what might happen to him that he played around and soon earned a wallop from the rasp. That was it. Poncho would have no more. Although a gentle man there is nothing untough or feeble about Merv Bennett, but he knew he was beaten. It was a week before he could win enough trust from the horse to approach him again with the idea of shoeing him.

In that incident Poncho showed exactly the fabric of which he is made. He will try his hardest to please, but if he does not understand or if something frightens him, he loses all his threads of confidence and co-operation.

With his wide, endearing black eyes, Poncho looked as if he wanted to be loved more than anything else in the world. Because the only humans he had known had given him a tough time, and because his sensitivity to such was somewhat over-developed, he could not bring himself to give anyone a chance to show him affection. It took Ann four months before he would even accept a sugarlump out of her hand.

Each morning at 6.30, Merv rode his young horse five miles to work. Poncho needed so much education and introduction to life that tying him up all day on the road-side with a feed while Merv worked manufacturing concrete septic tanks, was at least a way to accustom him to traffic and the outside world. In the evenings he was ridden home, jumping logs and boundary fences on the way.

Merv was not impressed with the horse's gallop. He did not seem interested in moving fast and would only lob along. His steps were small and round, he never pulled and he never galloped up onto the bit. Merv had to admit that, thoroughbred or not, he was a slow horse; he would never be fast enough for what was needed. He could jump though, and he was as sharp and quick-witted as a fox. Riding him through bushland was an experience. He never missed a thing: any movement he would notice; at anything unusual he would leap into the air. If he stood on one end of a twig and the other end sprang up in front of him he would stop immediately and run back. Maybe he had stepped on the tail of a black snake when he was working the stock. A kangaroo, however, could appear almost under his nose and he would remain quite unconcerned; he was well used to them.

An introduction to cross-country, 1977.

As his strength increased so he began jumping more and more of the cross-country obstacles the Bennetts had constructed around their home. He was particularly adept in how he tackled the river at full speed. Galloping to the edge of the near-vertical descent, Poncho would pull himself up short on the brink, slide down on his hocks, pop into the river, turn sharp left over a log, sharp right and bound up the opposite bank. Where other horses fumbled he never made a mistake, so surefooted was he and so quick to assess a situation.

Although he was small and slow-paced, with inherent mental and physical problems in dressage, he could jump and he was clever. The Bennetts decided to aim him for the Melbourne Intermediate Three-Day Event in October of that year, 1977.

All the Bennett horses included the word 'Regal' in their name. Remembering the incident in Montreal involving his breeder, they named the scant brown horse Regal Realm.

ABOVE: Learning about show-jumping, 1977. BELOW: Although he measured 16 hh, Poncho rode like a tiny horse. Merv's chin is remarkably near Poncho's ears.

While Regal Realm was learning to adapt to a completely new life, a seventeen-year-old boy from Brisbane invested four hundred dollars in a flea-bitten grey seven-year-old. The horse had become bored of his life as a buck-jumper in a Queensland rodeo and been passed to a dealer. The boy had started riding only two years before.

With comparatively few one-day events throughout Australia young horses materialise at three-day events very quickly, albeit that some of the three-day events are of Novice or Intermediate standard.

Within ten months of leaving the station on which he was bred, Regal Realm found himself first near Sydney at the Hawkesbury One-Day Event and then at the Melbourne Intermediate Three-Day Event. Despite his masterly handling of the river-jump at his home, he had no such confidence in strange surroundings. At Hawkesbury a dammed-up piece of water unexpectedly following a log, made the newcomer do his best to refuse. He saw the water too late to stop. Instead he jumped across the log skewing to the side so that on landing he momentarily gripped the face of the bank with all four feet, like a fly on a wall. He could not keep his balance, and inevitably he slipped down into the water, regaining control of his legs as he did so.

He did not trust such places; possibly he had once become stuck in a bog or in the muddy edge of one of the drinking dams in the North.

At the Melbourne Three-Day Event a similar small log edged the corner of a lake. On the far side, in the water, was a tiny island no more than three feet across. After one refusal and a reminder with the whip, Poncho gathered himself together, sprang over the log and landed all four feet at once on the tiny island. Balancing

Regal Realm jumping with more power in 1978.

thereon for a few seconds he soon had to take a stride into the lake in order to save himself from a nose-dive.

The following April found Regal Realm stabled on the Sydney showground next to the flea-bitten grey buck-jumper from Brisbane.

David Green had never met any of the riders he was competing against in the Sydney Three-Day Event in the spring of 1978. Queenslanders rarely made the journey south and those from southern states rarely travelled all the way up to Queensland. Merv Bennett gave what assistance he could to this eighteen-year-old stranger to the eventing scene. He walked the course with him and helped him with his timings for the roads and tracks and steeplechase. Not all the old-timers were pleased to see a Queenslander do so well in his first three-day event. Merv was delighted; he saw much talent in David. He and Swift Deal were fourth in the Intermediate section and won the Best Under-Twenty-One prize.

Twelve thousand miles away 1977 had proved to be an extra-ordinary year in my life. My father had died in August after fighting cancer of the liver for a year. Elaine Straker's George had won for me both Badminton and Burghley, the latter being the European Championships that year. Village Gossip had been second at both German and Dutch Championships. Charles Cyzer's Killaire had been third at both Badminton and the USA Championships.

With the onset of 1978 everything seemed fine on the surface. I had been incredibly lucky to become the first eventer to be fully commercially sponsored, as Overseas Containers Ltd promised to underwrite my expenses up to the Moscow Olympics. Until it happened to me I was not fully aware of the magnitude of responsibility that sponsorship hoists onto the recipient. Suddenly an international company had put a great deal of money behind me in order to help pave my way to the Olympics. There was no Be Fair and no George to help with this responsibility. Both had retired. Apart from several of my own young horses that were renamed with the OCL 'Bay' suffix, there remained only Killaire and Village Gossip as top-class horses. Killaire did not run in OCL's name, which left only Gossip, temporarily leased to them, to wave the OCL flag. Despite his two second places in 1977, Gossip was as difficult an individual to ride as he was brilliantly fast and clever over his fences. I had to do so little wrong, for him to lose confidence in me and apply the brakes in front of a fence. Gossip's first attempt at Badminton posed a genuine threat to our combined abilities.

With a strong hand from the Almighty we did not let our new sponsors down at Badminton: Gossip ran second to Jane Holderness-Roddam and Warrior.

In September of that year Gossip and I experienced the World Championships in 90°F and 99 per cent humidity at Lexington, Kentucky. Gossip would never perform well across country unless he was allowed to go at his own pace. That pace was full gallop. Gossip fell six fences from home, through exhaustion alone.

Being number one to go for the British team, I was left with no option but to pick Gossip up and push and shove him around the remainder of the course to the finish.

Such an experience left me increasingly less enthusiastic about

Triumph is just 'umph' added to 'try': Killaire, whose middle name was 'Try', wins Badminton, 1979. (*Findlay Davidson*)

my sport. It made me question even more seriously why we all struggle to represent our country in a team event. Three-day eventing is principally an individual sport; is it wise to subject horses to a decision made by their riders possibly at a time when they are forced to think of their team before their horse?

A year later, in 1979, Killaire won Badminton while Gossip's uninspired round showed he needed an easy year in order to recover from Lexington. OCL provided the capital to buy one horse in an effort to ensure that I would not be relying solely on Gossip for the Olympics, who, by Moscow, would be twelve and with six years of heavy competition behind him. The New Zealand horse, Bandolier, now Mairangi Bay, became the insurance policy. Bought immediately after Lexington where he had competed, it was then too early to know that only two horses out of all those that took part in the World Championships were to show any consistent form again. Those two were American Jimmy Wofford's Carawich, and Village Gossip.

In June 1979 I finished writing *Four Square*,* a book based on the exceptional and peculiar stories attached to each of the four horses that had won Badminton for me. Two months later the fourth side of the square, Killaire, missed a medal in the European Championships at Luhmühlen. The rides he gave me on the steeplechase and cross-country course made his victorious Badminton efforts feel ordinary. That evening a deep bruising, or bursitis, developed which pressed on the navicular bone in his foot and rendered him acutely lame for several months. He was withdrawn from the Championships when lying third.

The inspiration and enthusiasm that symbolised our completely amateur, family association with Be Fair's career, faded fast when his progress was abruptly ended at the 1976 Olympics. A year later, following the death of my father, a generator of motivation, such spirits were finally submerged.

Often I asked myself why I continued eventing when it was no longer the fun it used to be. For me and for others too, there has to be infinitely more than materialistic aims. It was not a difficult question to answer. I loved horses and I loved the thrilling challenge of developing a confidence with them which could withstand the highest tests of mutual trust, in the form of a demanding cross-country course. If I wanted to continue pursuing these loves then I would have to accept that things had changed and it was no longer possible to enjoy it in the same way as in previous years.

Such an acceptance, along with a number of injuries to my horses during those three years, gave rise to a small but deep-rooted feeling of despair late in 1979. Self-destruction is well nourished by despair.

* Pelham Books, 1980.

The 1979 Sydney Three-Day Event, after the dressage phase. The year-of-birth brand is clearly seen on Regal Realm's quarters. (*Ann Bennett*)

In October 1979 the Australians held their selection trials at the Melbourne Three-Day Event for the 1980 Moscow Olympics.

Merv Bennett won them on his Montreal hero, Regal Reign. Regal Realm, competing in his fourth three-day event was second, despite a run out at a corner fence in a combination. He was put on the Moscow Olympic short-list as Merv's reserve horse, along with Regal Melody. Such was the ferocity of the third fence at Melbourne that only six completed the cross-country course and only three of those were clear – Merv Bennett and David Green. Despite a lapse in the show-jumping the following day David also found himself on the short-list for the Olympics. David was particularly surprised because four months earlier, having been fourth at Gawler, Australia's premier three-day event, he had been asked

whether Swift Deal could go to Moscow without him as he was too young and inexperienced. His joy lasted for three weeks. After the official vetting a ring-bone behind, that Swift Deal had owned for as long as David had known him, threw them out of the Olympics and back into Queensland.

That November, I made my first all-expenses-paid trip to the southern hemisphere. A person whom I had never heard from before, Jill Rymill of Adelaide, had written on the off-chance that I would like to go out to Australia and take some instructional clinics; perhaps she had heard that travelling was my favourite hobby.

In Australia I took a five-day clinic in Melbourne and a similar one with an evening lecture in Adelaide. This was followed by a visit to Sydney, where I gave what was probably my most successful talk to date and where an enthusiastic audience kept questions flowing for one and a half hours. After all that and a busy year I was ready for a few weeks' holiday. I barely recall a young man coming up to me at the end of the evening in Sydney, explaining that he had been dropped from the Olympic squad but hoped he could come to England for the next Badminton. Did I know where he could stay? I remember saying I was sure I could find somewhere, and if he did decide to come over, to give me a ring in the New Year and I would try and help him. I also remember hoping it was another of those many requests that would come to nothing.

David Green and Swift Deal competing in the Gawler Three-Day Event, South Australia, 1979.

On December 27th 1979, the Russians invaded Afghanistan. In seven months' time they expected the rest of the world to come and play games in their back garden, and by so doing unconsciously place a seal of approval on the Russian aggression. I was incensed, as were many others, and saw every reason why we should not partake in the Olympic Games. The Russians had over-run Afghanistan reportedly with eighteen divisions. This was no political light opera, it was a fully instrumented concert of frightening proportions and with world-wide consequences. I came up against many friends who did not feel that sport should be mixed with politics. I thoroughly agreed, but felt that such an ideology on this occasion had been heavily outweighed.

The Olympic Games, I cannot help feeling, have hit a sad but inevitable watershed. Progress, by the very nature of the word, means we cannot stand still. The Olympic ideals are outdated. No longer are we seeing a fieldful of pure amateurs. That would be impossible, for to be at the top of almost any sport these days requires serious and time-consuming training.

Particularly in the Iron Curtain countries, but in others too, sport is becoming a medium for the politician. In this new and highly technological age, a peaceful and non-political Olympic Games is, I fear, expecting a great deal. For it is one occasion when the world gathers together and where the television cameras from all over the globe are beamed into one place at the same time. It is a stage that the whole world can see at once. The Olympic Games have become yet another political theatre. The athletes, who should be playing the leading rôles, have instead merely become footlights illuminating the strifes of nations.

Six days after returning from Australia in the New Year of 1980

I hunted Be Fair. At seventeen he was loving his Leicestershire winters with my wonderful friends, Joss and Rozzie Hanbury. Half way through an excellent and fence-leaping day with the Belvoir, Be Fair landed too steeply over a big hedge. There was a crack like the sound of a stone bouncing off tarmac and within a stride Be Fair was standing still. As I led him back across the field to the roadway, he fumbled and stumbled in obvious and acute pain. It reminded me of his beastly experience in Montreal two and a half years earlier.

Remorse flooded in because I felt sure that if only I had kicked into the fence, instead of sitting still, he would have put in a bigger, faster leap whose trajectory would not have landed him at such a vertical angle. With front legs that never once gave any trouble in all ten years that we lived each other's lives, I could hardly believe that because of me he had finally and suddenly ruptured nearly everything that he could in his near-foreleg.

Harbouring this guilt and with the certain knowledge that the Afghanistan tragedy would be the start of much public and private cross-examination of Olympic candidates, I headed for Germany.

For the third time I had the envied opportunity to spend three weeks under one of Germany's top professional dressage exponents, Herbert Rehbein. After Montreal Alwin Schockemöhle had offered his sympathies and his help. Through his father-in-law, Otto Schulte-Fröhlinde, who owned the magnificent establishment in which Herbert worked, I found myself and two horses invited to stay at Grönwohld. Mercifully I also found Brigid Maxwell there when I arrived. She had worked with Herbert for five years and without her I would have gleaned little, as neither Herbert nor I spoke the other's language.

One afternoon early in my stay I was chewing over the Olympic problem whilst grooming one of my two horses, Botany Bay. The internal public address system tuned in and announced that there was a person-to-person telephone call for me from Australia. I dropped my brush and scampered off to the office. I could not think who would be ringing from Australia, and in obvious urgency if they had tracked me down fifty miles north of Hamburg.

It was David Green, informing me that he and his horse were coming over for Badminton and did I know of anywhere they could stay. Not only by then could I not remember what this Australian

43

OPPOSITE: Be Fair, after winning the European Championships in Luhmühlen, 1975. His hunting injury filled me with remorse. He had done so much for me – in fact he had given me a life. (*Jürgen Gebhardt, Bild Zeitung*)

ABOVE: Botany Bay in training at Grönwohld, near Hamburg, under Herbert Rehbein, January, 1980. (*Heiner Köpcke*)

Herbert Rehbein, top professional dressage exponent. Grönwohld, 1980.
(*Heiner Köpcke*)

looked like, but also I had forgotten his name and by the end
of the conversation called him Peter. Not knowing what to say
I told him I would have a think and he was to ring me back in
Germany in a fortnight.

Whether it was because my mind was involved in the pros and
cons of going to Moscow, or deep into dressage, or a bit of both,
I do not know, but the call from Australia slipped my mind. When
the second one came, in two weeks' time, I was caught short. I
was not at all sure we wanted a stranger at home. We are very
particular about whom we have to stay at Appleshaw, because the
wrong attitude from one person can squeeze lemon-juice over
everything. However, I felt obliged to say that we would definitely
be able to find him somewhere although I rather doubted we would
have room ourselves.

To my head girl, Lisa, I left the decision of whether or not to risk having this David Green with us at home. It was she, I felt, who would bear the worst consequences if the Australian was not a success. A few days later I wrote to Brisbane informing David that he was welcome to come and stay at Appleshaw until Badminton, but I could not guarantee him a roost after that.

In this way we would have to suffer for only two months if we did not like him.

Meanwhile the media were carefully cooking to boiling point the dilemma of boycotting Moscow. I cared deeply and tried in vain to beat up support from athletes in a variety of sports. I made many telephone calls and was rarely met with a straight answer. The normal line was an escape chute, 'Well, what real good will it do to the situation if we don't go?' Just as the answer to that was incalculable, so was the answer to how much good it would do the Kremlin if we all went to Moscow and were thereby seen to be supporting subversive aggression.

The most I could manage was to make my own stand, which, much to the displeasure of my nerves, eventuated in my being asked to appear on BBC's 'Nationwide' one evening.

Richard Meade, triple gold medallist and fulcrum of most of our international teams for two decades, felt as strongly as I did – but in reverse. It is a tribute to friendship that Richard and I remained without hostility despite our completely opposed views.

Glancing through the kitchen window as I came into the house one cold February evening, I saw briefly a blond man with a moustache sitting at the kitchen table, talking to Lisa. Momentarily wondering who Lisa's new friend was, I walked into the kitchen to make sure everything was all right with the horses since I had just returned from a trip to London.

Lisa introduced the man as David Green. I could not believe what I saw. My dim memory told me to expect a small brown-haired youth, not someone six feet tall with a mass of blond hair and a dreadful moustache to match.

The moustache lasted only a few days and David's chances of riding his brilliant acrobatic horse at the 1980 Badminton Horse Trials, a few weeks.

Swift Deal had been like Be Fair, never a day of lameness. David was horrified at my suggestion that he should enter for the Punchestown Three-Day Event in May in case something went wrong and they never reached Badminton in April. It had never occurred to him that anything could go wrong.

Two weeks before Badminton I arrived back from London early one morning to be greeted with the news that Swift had given himself a bruised leg while grazing in the field. He was lame. The pair had already proved themselves ready for the big challenge by convincingly completing two high-standard one-day events that spring. Their chances of competing at the event for which they had travelled from the other side of the world now looked slender.

Within a few days David's mother, father and sister were due to arrive in England for Badminton. They still came over. Swift's leg improved and he did the dressage test there. After a lengthy examination, Nipper Constance, our chief adviser on legs, and

Lunch in the kitchen. David and myself with two of the girls; Charlie Micklem, co-jockey at that time, is in the background. March 1980. (*Courtesy Riding magazine*)

always an optimist, advised David that it would be wiser not to run the horse on the hard going across country. The Australian pair were withdrawn.

It was only when things started to go so dreadfully wrong for David that I turned around and noticed him. The general gossip had, as usual, added two and two to make five and presumed that he and I were already good friends and going out together. He was only twenty, quiet and not an easy person with whom to familiarise. Unbeknown to the gossips I was enjoying at that time the company of a gentleman who worked in London.

Watching the manner in which David, and indeed his family too, coped with the biggest disappointment so far, made admiration for him grow from my sympathy.

ABOVE: David and Swift Deal, Badminton, 1980. (*Peter Ayres*)

OPPOSITE: Killaire nearly wins his second consecutive Badminton. A mistake at the water-jump on the final day relegated him to second place. April 1980. (*John Birt*)

Killaire very nearly won Badminton for a second year in succession. As it was, he chiselled his name deep into the book of records by being the only horse to have been first, second and third there. He was second to the New Zealander, Mark Todd, on Southern Comfort, his native mount of six weeks' acquaintance. Killaire gave me every chance to win. All we needed was a clear round in the show-jumping, a requirement which was no longer difficult for him. Inordinately well and cheeky at twelve years of age and at his third Badminton, he bounded into the arena and spooked quite obviously as he cantered past the water-jump. Instead of translating that spook into riding twice as strongly as usual when approaching that fence, I failed to take it into account. Killaire,

50

completely uncharacteristically, shuddered to a halt as he continued to play his game in front of the water. With a sharp reminder, he splashed into it instead of over it.

The Olympic hopes for the horse that OCL had purchased for me two years earlier in 1978, were deflated forever when Mairangi Bay broke down on the steeplechase at Badminton. Ever since we bought him after Lexington, we had been worried by almost every other part of him except his tough pony-legs. His general poor state of health and respiratory difficulties had occupied much of many experts' time. That he should now have a tendon problem as well seemed beyond credibility.

Mairangi and Beagle Bay – the latter purchased on behalf of OCL by Gossip's extremely unselfish owner, David Kingsley – were each bought for plenty enough money during the last two years. Both had been dismal disappointments and were rarely in a fit state for competition. In the back of my mind I felt it was divine justice. I had always believed that no one could buy himself to the top, but then I had been looking for horses in order to try and stay there and give my sponsors something worthy of their support. Somewhere there was a balance. I reckoned I must have missed it.

Village Gossip gave Charlie Micklem, my co-jockey for two years, a marvellous introduction to Badminton in 1980. Together they made a very tough course seem effortless. Charlie made the easy mistake of taking off with his weight a fraction of a second before Gossip did, at the second element of a bounce-fence near the finish. Even at that late stage in the course, Gossip, acutely sensitive to his rider's balance, could not tolerate it and refused.

A few weeks after Badminton Mairangi Bay went up to Nipper Constance for a tendon operation. Nipper, meanwhile, was very taken with the Australian horse, Swift Deal, and he was sufficiently involved in the disappointment which had enveloped him to offer to summer Swift for two months and keep his leg under observation. The only treatment he could recommend was ultrasonics as the horse was suffering from deep bruising of the tendon sheath and cannon bone. Hopes were high that Swift would be able to compete in a three-day event in the autumn.

Shortly before Badminton 1980 the British Equestrian Federation announced that they would support Mrs Thatcher's plea by sending no teams to the Moscow Olympics. All the major equestrian nations rallied in agreement.

By then the Australians were in team training, preparing for their trip to Europe and subsequently the Olympic Games.

Merv Bennett had already bought air tickets for his wife and children to travel via England to Moscow.

As soon as the Australian Government gave its lead by preferring its athletes not to support the Russians, Merv took his horses home and turned them out. He then put down a deposit on two hundred and fifty acres of land adjoining his own; previously he had been wondering whether or not he could afford the purchase.

A few days later rumours of an alternative equestrian Olympics filtered across Australia.

Eventually it was confirmed that the French had agreed to stage a major World Championships at their *école militaire* in Fontaine-bleau.

Merv Bennett then knew for certain that he would have to sell either Regal Reign or Regal Realm before he left Europe. He was not going to the other side of the world without his family, he had committed himself to buying two hundred and fifty acres of land, and he never saw any rebate from the air-line tickets to Moscow.

David and I disappeared into Ireland in mid-May in search of young horses, optimistically hoping that our relationship was developing unnoticed. I went to great lengths to cover our tracks, determined that no one should know. My desire for secrecy was twofold. Firstly, I have an instinct for privacy in such matters. Secondly, I was afraid of what even my closest friends might think of me for going out with someone who had come to Appleshaw as a working pupil and, worse still, was only twenty years old. Bound by tradition I have always believed that if one of a couple is six years older, it should be the man. Disappointingly few people seemed unaware of our relationship although it was not until July that my mother noticed that both David and I were having the same day off each week.

After a frustrating week trying and failing to discover young talented horses, David went up to Belfast to spend a month riding every sort of proposition for Harold Lusk, a big-time international horse dealer.

Meanwhile I made my way home to pack up for another trip to Australia. The Committee of the Gawler Three-Day Event had asked me out as a promotional medium, to ride in their South Australian Championships at the beginning of June. Before leaving home a decision that for some years I had anticipated with dread, loomed close.

Be Fair's leg was not mending well. In the short time that I had been in Ireland, his hunting injury seemed to have deteriorated, his discomfort increased. He was living in a field with Gossip and a young horse. He limped away when Gossip bit him on the bottom; he was no longer interested in playing games. Neither did he seem to want to have much to do with me; he was no longer a proud horse, his image of himself was shattered.

The day before my flight to Australia, Nipper Constance came to see his leg. He put a pain relieving injection into it, the effects of which would last for a few weeks. Never a person to leave someone in indecision, Nipper told me that there was really only one suitable place left for Be Fair.

For a time I could not accept it. After talking to no one else but myself from Heathrow to Singapore, gradually my mind lessened its rejection of the inevitable.

On the last leg of the flight to Adelaide I wrote home to my mother, asking her if she could make sure Be Fair was in Heaven by the time I returned. Selfishly, I wanted to be as far away as possible when Be Fair lay down for the last time.

It was asking much, for my mother was as involved in our deep love for Be Fair as my father had been. She would be severing a last link with her husband too.

A grey mare called Orcades, on regular duty with the South Australian police, was to be my mount for the Intermediate section of the Gawler Three-Day Event.

She looked to be an athletic thoroughbred type with a kind, wise eye. She appeared powerful and fast. Having rapidly discovered that dressage was not her forte I looked forward to jumping her. It soon became evident that despite all her visible assets, she lacked something crucial – a jump. The police had told me

Orcades. The Australian Championships, Gawler Three-Day Event, 1980. (*Delamere Usher*)

that she was not too special with her near-fore and so it proved to be. Out of thirty fences on the cross-country course she managed not to hit four of them. During our one and a quarter hours together in the speed and endurance phase, I had no control whatsoever on the first circuit of the steeplechase; on the cross-country I fell off once, and nearly oh, so nearly, twice; had four refusals and ninety time penalties. The press loved it, the gate increased by forty per cent, both Orcades and I were still alive and therefore I reckoned my air-fare was well earned.

Orcades on Phase B. She was out of control and jumped flat and low all the way; it was fortunate the steeplechase fences were so small. (*Delamere Usher*)

Three weeks later David collected me from Heathrow. Nearing home he said how sorry he was about Be Fair. Knowing that he had read *Up, Up and Away*,* the book I wrote in honour of that great horse, I imagined therefore he understood what a huge loss it was.

Appleshaw seemed an infinitely lonelier place. It mattered not in the least that my incredible chestnut had been retired for four years, his character and personality were of such standing that he left a stark hole. That evening I went for a walk around our fields with my little Cavalier King Charles Spaniel, Oliver Plum, trying to adjust to the fact that wherever I looked I would never find Be Fair again.

* Pelham Books, 1978.

On the dressing table in my bedroom was a note from my mother, assuring me that things had gone all right the week before. She had brought Be Fair in from the field in the morning and given him a feed in his own exalted stable. All his depression fell away as he became convinced that he was going to start work again and life began to offer him renewed purpose.

Later she had fed him a whole packet of Polos as our vet, Paul Farringdon, arrived. Then she kissed Be Fair good-bye, stepped into her car and fled to the downs for the remainder of the day.

AN ANCIENT BEDOUIN LEGEND

When God decided to create the horse, he spoke to the South Wind and said, 'I wish to create from you a being who shall be the glory of my faithful and the terror of my enemies!' The wind answered, 'Lord, I listen and obey.' Then God took a handful of wind and fashioned from it a chestnut horse. He said, 'Lo, I have created the horse. I have moulded it from the wind, I have tied Good Fortune to its mane. It will fly without wings. It will be the noblest of animals. Equal in pursuit as in evasion, it will carry those who will praise, exalt and glorify My Name!' God then blessed the horse with the sign of glory and happiness, marking its forehead with a star. And the horse leapt into space.

En route to the alternative Olympics in August, the Australian squad of Merv Bennett and Wayne Roycroft each with two horses, and Philippa Glennon with one, arrived in England in mid-July. They all stayed together in a cottage and their horses were stabled at John Sheddon's in Gloucestershire. The fourth member of their team, Andrew Hoy, was already in England learning and competing with Mark Phillips.

Regal Realm had his first outing on English turf at Molland in Devon a few weeks later. Until then the little horse had never pulled. He had always been the type that had to be kicked along and made to attack his fences. Merv found aggressive riding particularly necessary when approaching any drop fences, as Poncho would jump too precisely up and down and thereby land too steeply.

Suddenly Regal Realm became extremely difficult to control at Molland. Whether it was because the malformed eye-tooth had been found and extricated shortly before leaving his home, or whether it was the change in hemisphere or the fact that after four years he at last felt at his full strength it is impossible to tell. With one run out, he pulled and tanked his way up and down and in and out of the twisty, hilly cross-country course.

It was in July of 1980 that Foxy Bubble first arrived at Appleshaw. He was owned by the British Equestrian Federation and had been halfway round Badminton and all the way around Punchestown with Jane Holderness-Roddam. She was giving up three-day eventing and Foxy was left without a jockey. To my delight and flattery the Federation asked me to ride him at Burghley.

With a moderate performance at our first one-day event together followed by an ear-splitting display as he crashed his way around the One-Day Event Championships at Locko, I perceived that Foxy Bubble was possibly not quite my horse. He was 16.3 hh, strong and very gangly; even though he portrayed undoubted elegance, he felt as if he was a man's ride.

By August, with Killaire, Gossip and Foxy Bubble fit and well, our plans were almost complete to face the intricate challenge of riding three horses in three different countries in three three-day events held on three consecutive weekends.

Killaire was nominated to join the British team for Fontaine-bleau, Gossip would travel as reserve and so would a borrowed trailer attached to my unsuspecting Audi. Once we were finished in France, I would drive Gossip in the trailer to Germany for Luhmühlen, returning just in time to ride the unfortunate Foxy Bubble at Burghley.

The principal problems about this scheme were spare tack and my fitness. For every horse that is running in a three-day event we always make certain we have spares of everything for him. This is normally no hassle, but our present plan meant that we would need to double up on many things, as there wouldn't be time between events to transfer and check them all. My fitness was another worry. Over the past year since that thread of destructive despair had taken root I had allowed myself to become fatter and sloppier. For the last month before Fontainebleau I adopted a personal torture routine of 6 a.m. runs followed immediately by three-hundred skips, once my legs had de-rubberised from the run. I have always skipped for fitness, but running is something I hate and, like swimming underwater, I can last for only a very short time. A mile with one steep hill was the maximum distance achieved.

When Killaire went lame behind the day before we were due to leave for Fontainebleau, our hopes of the triple attack went with him. In retrospect I am not altogether sure that this was not a leniency of Fate. Killaire was prevented from enjoying the curtain-call to his career at the alternative Olympics by the most futile of incidents. A few weeks earlier he had stuck his hindleg through the wooden wall of his stable while rolling. He slightly bruised the back of his hock and at the time it seemed inconsequential. After a few easy days he resumed work. Only at the very end of his training did it become evident that the Achilles tendon must have caught the worst of the bruising. The small bump reappeared three inches below the point of the hock and he became very lame.

Gossip was back in the number one spot. He would be with the British team the next day when, on account of the French fishermen's blockade of all their ports, the horses travelled by a specially chartered aircraft to Paris.

We had not competed together for a year and a half. Our last joint venture was Badminton in 1979 when, as a result of Lexington, Gossip was not enjoying himself. I had, however, ridden him at home for the last two months as he was the official team reserve horse.

Neither Charlie nor I could make any sense of Gossip's dressage, and I deemed it best not to tackle it any more. Trying to sort it out upset us both and a passive attitude to him would at least leave us mentally fresh for the challenge of the Olympic-calibre cross-country course that faced us in Fontainebleau.

Trotting Gossip at his own insistently speedy pace twice around a six-mile ride through a French forest left him no more biddable before his dressage. Shortly before our test my mind had a blank and couldn't remember if we should rein-back five or six paces. Ernst Bachinger, our team dressage trainer from Vienna, who had not been able to fathom Gossip either, drily replied, 'It doesn't really matter how many steps, does it?'

Asking virtually nothing from Gossip in order that he would not become rigid in both his body and his brain, we endured our test. He did not tense up but he did little else either and we earned a mark that left us sixty-fifth out of the sixty-nine starters.

David came to France to watch. He had the opportunity to compete as an individual as each country could enter six riders and Australia had sent over only four. A second disappointment manifested itself when after his first autumn event it became obvious that Swift's leg was going to need much more time to heal completely.

With our dressage test and final cross-country course-walk completed there was not much to do on the afternoon preceding the big day. David and I happened to wander past the dressage arena as a small, stringy, ewe-necked horse, ridden by an equally stringy but tall man, was attempting his test. David recognised

Regal Realm and Merv Bennett perform their dressage at Fontainebleau, 1980. The bulge on the underside of Poncho's neck indicates that he is resisting the contact and hollowing his back against any pressure on the bit. (*Hugo Czerny*, above; *Findlay Davidson*, below)

Village Gossip exhibiting much the same problems as Regal Realm in the dressage. Fontainebleau, 1980. (*Jim Bennett*)

the pair as Merv Bennett and Regal Realm. There were moments during the test, in between holding his neck like a goose and taking staccato steps, when it was almost possible to imagine that this rabbity little horse could one day perform a reasonable test. Knowing his background as I do now, it was remarkable that Merv was able to produce then what he did. Seeing the horse for the first time in the Fontainebleau arena, and knowing nothing of his past, left me with little enthusiasm for him. One Gossip was enough, and Regal Realm's mark was only four better than his. David assured me I was wrong to be so scathing, he had seen him go extremely well across country in Australia. No more was either said or thought about Regal Realm.

The British team did not complete Fontainebleau. Chris Collins retired with concussion and Richard Meade's horse produced azoturia (a muscle cramp) at the end of Phase C, the roads and tracks.

With his own unique brand of scintillating rounds in both cross-country and show-jumping, Gossip pulled himself up fifty-eight places to seventh position at the end of the three days.

Once again, as he had done at Badminton in 1978, Gossip rescued me from the edge of a cliff and galloped me back into the land of hope. By the time Fontainebleau arrived I was hanging on by the thinnest shred of confidence, for much had gone wrong in the past two years. I had begun to feel that all I had built in the shape of a career over the last decade was slipping away beyond my clutch, as my riding seemed to worsen and more horses went lame. To Gossip I owed a debt of gratitude.

I bought Regal Realm because he jumped and ran away like Village Gossip.

Village Gossip, suspicious of what lies beneath this big drop table fence, inspects it rather too closely. His over-cautiousness forced him to bank the top of the fence but his marvellous balance kept him upright. (*Hugo Czerny*)

Gossip jumps a speedy and accurate round in a bitless bridle, a pre-war invention. He pulled so hard across country that, no matter how soft the bit, he would cut the corners of his mouth. He therefore appreciated wearing no bit at all the following day. Interestingly Gossip could not tolerate a Hackamore (the more usual form of bitless bridle), but he accepted this old design, which operated more like a double bridle. Fontainebleau, 1980.

At twelve years old Gossip and Killaire must soon retire. Both Mairangi and Beagle Bay had soundness problems and the most recent addition, Foxy Bubble, did not look like being my ride for much longer. Botany Bay had always had weak legs, his soundness was therefore also questionable. Any youngsters we had were too inexperienced to break into the three-day event scene for several years to come. Once again we were faced with no horse for the

64

future and nothing for OCL to support in the 1982 World Championships. They had generously agreed to sponsor me for a further two years following 1980. In the hopes that I might burgle a little capital from them, I had been looking for an Intermediate horse all year. Regal Realm's stage and age fitted the requirements well. However, from what little I had seen of him he was not my idea of the sought-after horse.

Entirely through David's repeated persuasion, after the final veterinary inspection preceding the show-jumping phase at Fontainebleau, we went to have a look at the Australian horses that were for sale. The only horse that was not priced at around £20,000 was Regal Realm. This was partly on account of his size and partly because, as Merv's reserve horse, he had been withdrawn after the dressage and therefore had not publicly proved himself across country. The fact that he had not run held my interest. Such a demanding course as Fontainebleau would have taken a fair chunk out of the length of any horse's competitive life.

As I approached Regal Realm, a large Canadian was terminating his acquaintance with the horse, saying he was definitely too small. He was small. Standing next to him he seemed little higher than a pony. In fact his withers did come up to the same place on my nose as Gossip's, but there was no breadth or substance to this horse to indicate that he was 16 hands.

To ride him was like sitting on the proverbial knife. He was so narrow that I could barely keep my weight central and if I did not, he veered sharply to whichever side my balance moved. With his head held high in the air, any chance of doing some dressage to see how he felt was out of the question. Instead I began to jump him. It was like being transported by a four-legged dynamo. The feel of elasticity he gave was exceptional, but to stay on top of him was difficult. The huge power which came from behind, cannoned me onto his short vertical neck from a saddle that sat high up on his shoulders.

There were no practice cross-country fences to test his boldness and yet I could not be responsible for spending so much money on a horse who may be chicken. Much to the horror of the English *chef d'équipe*, who wanted me in one piece for the show-jumping that afternoon, and much to the displeasure of Bill Roycroft, the Australian *chef*, at my taking such a liberty, we headed for the

65

Bill Roycroft, veteran of five Olympic Games. (*Stuart Newsham*)

crowd-barriers. These were the movable type which stood about four feet high, manufactured of vertical grey steel bars in six-feet long sections which linked together. Regal Realm bounced over these and, once he realised he was outside the boring confines of the practice arena, he took off. Dust spat up as we shot down the main sand track between the stables; only by heading him for a part of the forest that had not been cleared was I able to regain some control. Turning him back and still battling with him, I thought I had better see how he coped with a fence at speed. It sounds reckless, but buying a horse, particularly an expensive one, is a big responsibility; it is necessary to find out as much as possible with the limited facilities available. At a fair pace we headed back

Dick Stillwell, trainer and adviser to many national and international competitors over the last two decades. (*John Birt*)

towards the row of crowd-barriers. There were some mirthless faces as we arrived in the practice arena covered in sand and highly delighted. Merv did not mind, he knew his horse's capabilities.

Dick Stillwell, a long-time adviser, my mother, David and I discussed the horse for a brief moment. It can take years to find a horse with star quality; a great many people in several countries are searching all the time. There are very few extra special horses in the world but between us we thought Regal Realm may be one of them. Subject to a clean bill of health we agreed to buy him.

In under half an hour we had come to a decision that was to build the future in an unforeseeable shape.

At that point Merv's first horse, Regal Reign, was taken off the market. Although he would have fetched double the price of his small neighbour, neither of the Bennetts really wanted to sell him. He was more suited to Merv's size and was a very much faster horse than Regal Realm.

Merv felt that in truth Regal Realm was a girl's horse who seemed to respond better to his sixteen-year-old daughter, Jodie. Nonetheless Merv still felt uncomfortable about selling the horse because he had originally been given him by a man who had worked tirelessly for the promotion and benefit of the sport in Australia from its embryonic days. Sir Alec Creswick had, however, always said that Merv was free to do what he wanted with Regal Realm; if he sold him he expected a bottle of whisky.

A case of Chivas Regal arrived at Allanvale, Sir Alec's home, not long after Fontainebleau.

By the end of the substitute Olympics I had succeeded in persuading Richard Meade to ride Foxy Bubble at Burghley.

Having enjoyed the sputnik-style thinking and sharp athleticism of Gossip around Fontainebleau's stiff cross-country course, I could not imagine myself struggling to persuade the big, elongated and un-surefooted Foxy Bubble around even half a course like that. He definitely needed a man, someone who could hold him together and make certain that his engine was well under him as he came into each and every fence. Maybe, then, his obvious talents could be utilised.

At first it was thought to be a good idea. However, when I returned from France I found that there was a different attitude amongst members of the committee which was responsible to the British Equestrian Federation for the horses owned by that body. It was decided that I should ride Foxy through Burghley. The committee felt that if a change of jockey was made and the horse still went badly no real conclusion would be reached. No one would know whether a bad performance was due to the new partnership not having had time to settle down, or whether Foxy was just no good at the game. I was warned that this was Foxy's last chance and that if he did not make a better showing he would probably be sold.

By the time we arrived at Burghley, memories of the dreadful ride at Locko and of Foxy's inadequate ability to collect himself were beginning to occupy my mind. These increasing fears were heightened by a letter received from Foxy's Northumberland breeder, Colonel Cookson, a few days earlier. He wrote that as a yearling Foxy used to fall over his own legs whilst galloping down the hills past his house. He often thought, he wrote, that he would break his neck.

In desperation Foxy was asked to poke his nose through a double bridle, to see if that would give me any more say in the matter. He went so well on the flat that I tried him over some fences, with equally good results, but then he always went well when he was not in a competition. However, with the definite encouragement of my mother, who, having hunted all her early life in a double, felt that riding in a snaffle was like playing the piano with gloves on, I decided to try the new bridle in the competition itself.

Foxy did the same to me in the dressage phase as he did to Jane Holderness-Roddam when she rode him at Badminton in the spring. Once in the big arena, with its atmosphere of occasion, his mind seemed to explode. He strutted around with his head cocked, using an open-fronted tent on the corner of the arena as a reason for not standing still for one of the several five-second periods of immobility required.

Eventually, eight long minutes later, we jiggled and joggled out of the arena. As a small compensation for all the wrong doings, Foxy did show some tremendous movement. His mark, therefore, was nothing like as embarrassing as Gossip's at Fontainebleau despite a convincing display of his worst fault, lack of concentration.

My spirits for the next day were fast depleted by my diminishing courage. Memories of comments by Foxy's past critics, one of which I had always been, flooded in. 'A diplomatic illness' for the jockey was even suggested. But, for all that, I very much wanted to ride Foxy; it was a challenge and I had little to lose. I never felt my neck was in much greater danger than it was riding any other horse. I thought Foxy would have refusals and hit his fences, but I did not think we would fall. He had, after all, made a brilliant recovery at Locko when I had ridden on too long a stride and too fast into a fence, without appreciating that the take-off was boggy.

Never having jumped with two reins before, nor wanted to, we spent some time fixing up rubber reins of different colour and width for curb and bridoon. Hopefully, if I was in a muddle, a quick downward glance would tell me which one I was grabbing the tightest. When Foxy galloped at home he set his jaw and went, but he seemed to appreciate the feel of his new bridle and never

Foxy finishes the Burghley cross-country after an infinitely better round than we had dared to hope, 1980. (*John Birt*)

tried to tip onto his forehand and gallop away. In fact, I was so much in command on the steeplechase that I mis-timed it and collected four penalties.

The double bridle seemed to give him an added dimension of self-confidence and to my amazement Foxy jumped around Burghley in control and in style. I was as surprised as I was glad that the British Equestrian Federation had made me persevere with him. He finished ninth and shortly afterwards he was tucked up for a long winter holiday while I hoped that his performance was no fluke.

At Burghley I was already beginning to hear mumblings about the 'scratchy little mover' I had bought from the Australians. I was also reproached over the manner in which I had tried out the horse. Knowing his owner had agreed to my wish to jump the crowd-barriers, the rebukes met with little but humour. The mutterings concerning Regal Realm's limited movement did worry me though, because they were true. It was going to be an uphill struggle, if it was even possible, to bring about a change.

A short while after Burghley, Swift was once again invited by Nipper to winter with him and David flew back to Australia.

A few nights later, when I was not in the gayest of moods anyway, a respected friend telephoned and gave me a thorough sharpening up. He pinpointed how far I had let myself and my standards fall in the last two years; how I could not even turn myself out decently any more and how my figure had gone. Assuring me that many of my critics were having a mouthwatering time as they chewed over my unhindered decline, I was told that I had better mend my ways before it was too late. A mention was also made of that young layabout of an Australian I was wasting my time with. Although the carpet I stood on was momentarily pulled from under my feet, there was a great deal of truth in all that was bravely fired at me. It helped.

The next morning I went on a diet, but still I counted the days until that solitary month had passed and it was time for me to fly out, once again on an all-expenses-paid trip, to Australia to ride in the Melbourne Three-Day Event.

During that month Joanna Capjon and I spent many hours in discussion as to how we were going to tighten the draw-strings in every conceivable direction to make the New Year tick along with renewed incentive and order. After three years of devotion to Be Fair, Jo had left Appleshaw shortly after the Montreal Olympics. Lisa took her place and survived manfully for three and a half increasingly difficult years. Having experienced different countries and a variety of jobs, by accident Jo eventually landed back at Appleshaw. It is not always a good policy to re-employ, but she had grown up with Be Fair and me; we were both Scorpios and understood the other's weaknesses and strengths. Her return to managing my horses was an enormous stimulus to my confidence and happiness.

However talented a rider may be, he or she will find it extremely difficult to stay consistently at the top without a totally dedicated and reliable stage-manager. Every day of the year that we are with them, Jo and I check the horses' legs independently of each other.

Joanna, who returned to Appleshaw at the end of 1980. (*Stuart Newsham*)

We discuss what the other has noticed in the way of a little heat or filling, or a scratch somewhere, and decide if any action should be taken. Every evening Jo enters our remarks in a big diary, which is frequently useful when it is necessary to refer to a horse's health-history to decide how best to treat a problem. The old proverb, 'no foot, no horse', is keenly adhered to at Appleshaw. The best horse in the world is useless if he is not sound in all his limbs and healthy in every other way. It is the scrutinous attention to detail involved in the feeding, the amount of training and the monitoring of the condition of the horse's legs, that we believe is one of the cornerstones of success. Another lies in the horse's disposition. It is imperative that he is happy and enjoying every minute of his life if he is to give his best when his big day dawns. For this reason we like to turn each horse out in the field every day to graze and roll. We are also very particular whom we employ to care for them. The horses are normally the first to inform us if things are not running smoothly in the yard. They are extremely sensitive to atmosphere and a tense or unhappy one will produce a similar horse. One of the best rewards Joanna and I can receive does not glitter. It is instead the sight of contentment on the faces of our horses as they peer with interest over their stable doors during any normal working day. It is these faces and the warmth of the personalities behind them which make the work continue to be worthwhile even when something goes badly wrong.

Joanna's own experiences during her days at Appleshaw were sufficient to fill the paperback she wrote in 1982 called *Eventing Groom.**

OCL were adamant that they could supply no more capital to help finance the purchase of horses. I lived in hope that I would find a generous prospective owner to buy my Australian acquisition from me. At that point, to the disgust of my brother, Simon, who had painstakingly managed my shares for over a decade, I had vacuumed nearly all my own capital in buying this high-risk investment, Regal Realm. Accepting the criticism I could only pray that the small, brown thoroughbred was a 'lucky' horse. Many less talented than he had reached the heights by possessing such a quality.

Simon came home from the City at weekends and after Fontainebleau seldom forgot to enquire whether or not my crazy, irresponsible purchase had yet gone lame. On the third weekend he was brought up short. The answer was positive. I was forced to cease searching for a prospective owner until we discovered why

*Pelham Books, 1983.

he was lame and what we could do about it. Not long afterwards life played one of its many tricks when David Mason of the generous horse trials sponsors, the MacConnal-Mason Gallery, asked me if I knew of a first-class horse he could buy for me to ride. In my stables stood exactly the right horse. But how could I sell Regal Realm when he was unaccountably lame?

During the next month the little horse came sound and went lame at intervals. He also acquired a nasty cut on the pastern while he was in the field and another a millimetre above the eye while he was in the stable. Whenever the vet came to try and diagnose his problem Poncho would be mysteriously sound on that day. Eventually we took him to the Stratford back-man, Ronnie Longford, who manipulated his back, axis and fetlock joint, and after a week of slow work in straight lines, Poncho seemed all right. We then decided to give him a holiday over the winter.

A month later he caught a virus. His throat glands blew up, the glands under his tummy and in his sheath enlarged. His knee joints and his hocks swelled and the filling soon ran down his legs until it looked as if he stood on four bollards. Added to this he had a temperature and was covered in spots. He lost condition, what little there was to lose, but he survived. It appeared, however, that I had purchased an unlucky horse.

My brother had the gentleness to turn the whole dispiriting saga into a joke. Not that it was at all funny, but he knew that I had learnt my lesson the hard way, and our family has a habit of trying to find the funny side to whatever mishaps occur.

The Melbourne Three-Day Event was a welcomed success for me and an undoubted booster-injection of morale. By the time I arrived in Australia I was thin and fit. This was provident for soon I discovered that the two horses I was riding were facing their biggest test and both needed plenty of help across country. Olympic rider Brian Schrapel had trained Margaret O'Brian's Rippling Rumour for the duration of his eventing career. Despite some noisy punctuations to his cross-country round he was a good, bold horse and he won the Open class.

Jane Bailey, an old school friend who was pregnant at that time, owned Banco, a six-year-old having his first run in an Intermediate event. Despite climbing over the bogey fence, the coffin, leg by leg, he did himself credit and won his class.

OPPOSITE ABOVE: Rippling Rumour tackles a double-bounce combination downhill at the Melbourne Three-Day Event, 1980. The spacing between each of the three elements was four yards. Owing to the fence timber being so slender it was a difficult fence for the horse to judge as he approached.
OPPOSITE BELOW: Banco, the six-year-old who won the Intermediate class at Melbourne, 1980. (*Delamere Usher*)
ABOVE: Rippling Rumour jumps a clear round to win the Melbourne Three-Day Event. Bill Roycroft and St John Ambulance Australia watch.

David had managed to pick up a last-minute ride on Ernie Barker's Meenot, in the Intermediate. As they thundered off the two-mile steeplechase course and disappeared out of control at the same pace down Phase C, his cross-country promised to be entertaining.

Fortunately David regained the upper hand and Meenot was in better control by the time he had finished five miles of Phase C. Meenot said 'not' only once on the course and they finished a satisfactory eighth.

After the event David and I were destined to three weeks of combined teaching at the Victorian Equestrian Centre. Immediately this venture started off on the wrong leg. The organisers had kindly lent us an old BMW for the duration of our stay, but before we began the first day's teaching, a friend of David's smashed the car in a skid on a rain-lashed road. The ensuing weeks were filled with a kaleidoscope of different pupils. There were, I think, six three-day courses organised, with approximately fifteen people attending each course. However, we lived intrigued from day to day. Sometimes five people turned up, sometimes twenty-five. Some stayed two days, some stayed six. It was impossible to know exactly what was happening and after a while we carried on unbothered. During the second week I lost my voice and whispered my way through the remainder of the work.

A month's holiday followed in both Sydney and Brisbane. Then David and I re-emerged in another part of Melbourne where Paul Johnson had arranged two five-day clinics for us. These ran smoothly and were fun to do, though my voice disappeared again before they finished.

David and I were in a quandary. We shared an affinity that neither of us had experienced before. We very much wanted to be together but David's work as a fashion photographer was twelve thousand miles away from my career with horses. We thought we might solve this problem by marrying.

Such an idea sent shock-waves through our families. Although they both liked the opposite suitor, neither was quite the type the other had expected as a match for their offspring. They pleaded with us to give the relationship more time and reiterated our own fears that being married would not solve the problem. Reluctantly we agreed to spend twelve months apart, assessing the situation.

The Greens' telephone bill mounted to quadruple the normal sum; I was forced to put £200 towards ours. All this telephoning was in addition to a stream of letters chasing each other around the globe, and despite the fact that for three weeks I was not allowed to open my mouth even to whisper, after an operation to remove a cyst on my vocal chords.

Our agreement lasted three and a half months. Then David and I split the cost of a cheap ten-day return air ticket and he flew over to be with me at Badminton.

Nothing dramatic happened at Badminton in 1981. It was a reasonably straightforward course and not one over which either of my two slow horses, Killaire and Mairangi, could make good

David Hunt helps Mairangi Bay and myself work in for the dressage at Badminton, 1981. (*Jim Bennett*)

times. Killaire was tenth and Mairangi, although now sound but still not in maximum spirits, was placed twelfth. It was Killaire's final appearance in international eventing. Although only thirteen and very sound, he was never cut out to be more than a hunter. For four years he had plunged everything he possessed into becoming a record-breaker and earning his middle name of 'Try'. We wanted to retire him too soon rather than too late – that he had earned.

Three days later David flew back to Australia. Although lonely again, in a strange way I was happier than I had been for a very long time.

The following day was the Tidworth One-Day Event. Charlie, my co-jockey, was riding Poncho that spring in a few one-day events. We did not want to rush him towards the pressure of a three-day event until he had been given plenty of time to settle in and acclimatise. Tidworth was the pair's second outing. In an attempt to follow orders and take him easily across country Charlie had to fight to control him from start to finish. A bouncing brown bundle with his ears nearly in Charlie's mouth and a neck foaming with white sweat, tugged and yawed his way into sight and over the last eight fences of the course.

I knew how difficult he was to hold. On one occasion when cantering round a field at home, I tried to line him up for a fence in a dip under some trees, but was totally unable to influence his speed or direction. He is the only horse I have ridden who has managed to career straight past that fence without giving any indication that he knew I wanted him to jump it. It remained incomprehensible that small, sixteen-year-old Jodie Bennett had coped with him so easily in Australia.

Poncho was cooled off after his battle around Tidworth and returned to the horse-box. An hour later he was unloaded at home. He was hopping lame at the walk.

Similar to the lameness six months ago, there was nothing anywhere to show for it. On this occasion he was lame enough for long enough to nerve-block him. This is a diagnostic technique whereby an injection anaesthetises different parts of the leg. When the correct area is numbed the horse will trot up sound and it is therefore possible to pinpoint the locality of the injury. Poncho's trouble appeared to be in a front fetlock joint. A telephone call to his old home in Australia gave no clue to the problem. He had apparently always been a sound horse over there. We took him to see Nipper Constance who was not at all certain what was amiss, but he made an uncharacteristically gloomy forecast.

To pour hot water on to the burn, a bill then arrived from the English bloodstock agency that had landed the Australian horses ten months ago. It was the import duty on Regal Realm, and it amounted to £1,150. Not surprisingly in the circumstances, I did not have £1,150 hanging around, and I did not know how I was going to pay it. I was furious because I felt that this was a punch in the stomach that should have been delivered at the time I bought the horse as it increased his cost by over ten per cent. After brandishing my disgust around to a few, someone informed me that it was the importer who was liable to pay this duty. I was not the owner of Regal Realm when he was imported. I telephoned the bloodstock agency and informed them of their mistake. To my everlasting astonishment, they admitted no surprise and explained that they had thought it would be easier to obtain the money from me – 'with OCL sponsoring you' – than it would be to hassle someone on the other side of the world . . .

Since my problem horse had arrived, our own vet, Paul Farringdon, had taken a great interest in his curious lameness. When two weeks of ultrasonic treatment had produced little improvement he quietly ventured his own opinion and suggested a possible cure. By reading his X-rays Paul thought he could detect some very early signs of slight damage in the area of the fetlock joint. His successful treatment entailed replacing the joint fluid with an injection of synthetic joint-oil. The offending joint never changed shape; it remained normal throughout his lameness and throughout the four weeks he spent in one of our two rest and recuperation yards following the injection.

Foxy Bubble had assumed an OCL name and ownership by 1981 as the British Equestrian Federation no longer felt it wise to finance individual horses. Re-named Falmouth Bay he took on Punchestown in May with disappointing results. After one refusal and one run out it struck me that so poor was this horse's concentration and my methods of attracting it that we had better give him a really busy year, and adopt a 'make or break' attitude. Without his wits he would never make a top-class horse.

The day after Punchestown, Ireland's John Watson, Nils Haagensen (the Danish Fontainebleau victor) and I flew from Dublin to New York. Through a missed connection we arrived a day late in Kentucky, the heart of the USA. It had been a very long time since I went as mad as I did at Lexington.

Edith Conyers, who had her first taste of organising horse trials when she took on the World Championships in 1978, conceived the idea of an international invitation event and was not content until she had put it into practice.

She mustered $15,000 sponsorship from a number of generous individuals and flew in ten international riders from six countries.

The organising committee had pre-drawn the horses. Had the riders drawn straws for their prospective mounts, mine would have been the longest, and Australian Andrew Hoy's the shortest.

Richard Meade would not have drawn a very long one either. His partner was a huge Trakehner stallion who, throughout the time we were there, was continually driven away to serve his mares. During practice the horse impressed Ireland's John Watson to the extent that every time he passed an odd pile of wood chippings he asked whether or not Richard had been jumping nearby.

The day before we arrived, Mark Phillips had apparently spent the best part of four hours in a corner with a flea-bitten grey who insisted that for twelve years he had never dropped his head and was not going to start now. Eventually Mark's perseverance won and to his relief he found the horse was a good, bold jumper.

Germany's small, stout and friendly Harry Klugmann was on a pink Appaloosa of similar dimensions to himself. Rüdiger Schwarz and Helmut Rethemeier were both on big, striking, Germanic-looking horses. Nils Haagensen rode Edith Conyer's short-striding 15 hands dun horse who had competed only in Pony Club competitions.

Laser was my long straw, a beautiful bay thoroughbred kindly lent by his owner, Kim Whitehurst. In 1978 he had been well placed in many Open competitions with Mike Plumb, since when he had semi-retired. Mike had geared him up during the last two weeks before Lexington. He was definitely an old and stiff horse on the flat, but his jumping was something he loved. When eventually I understood how he best liked to be ridden he was a clean jumper too.

Laser loving his return to competition at the Rolex International Invitation Event at Lexington, Kentucky. (*Lynne Bruna*)

The Americans are in a class of their own when it comes to entertaining. With four solid nights of parties, it was fortuitous that we only had to ride a 'one-day event' that was spread over three days.

The extra enjoyment of Lexington '81, for my part, derived principally from having no attendant pressures. No one knew what was going to happen; nothing was expected of anyone, as none of us had our own horses. We were all there in the same dinghy and most of set sail, with the aid of an abundance of free food and drink, day and night.

Apart from Andrew Hoy and Helmut, who each had one fall, nothing alarming happened on cross-country day. Even Richard, who openly admitted his fear, completed with only two refusals.

Laser went superbly. I was warned that he stopped, but such was his enjoyment at returning to the job, and no doubt much encouraged by not being faced with massive fences, that he gave me a beautiful ride.

He behaved similarly the following day and, to the envy of most of the others, he won the prize for the best international: a gold and steel watch, presented by the United States equestrian team's new sponsors, Rolex. Moreover, it was a highly appreciated prize as my own watch had just broken irreparably and I was going to have to purchase one in the duty-free shop on my return journey.

My spirits shot into the elevator. My principal ambition is one day to be able to step onto any horse and feel how to ride him to the best of his ability in a matter of days as opposed to years. This goal has always held greater significance than that of ephemeral victories. The attraction of it lies in its infinity.

Both Melbourne and Kentucky had taken me a little closer to that distant objective. The morale boost of actually winning did not escape me either. There is a special feeling attached to having no one else in front. Apart from Melbourne, it was a sensation that had eluded me for twenty-five months.

Fair Deal completed his first three-day event at Gawler on the same weekend as Lexington. Barely six years old, David and I found this horse in a shed in Brisbane during our holiday six months earlier. We named him after our two most treasured horses. By then he had already seen two years on a racecourse and show-jumped to Grade B standard. After Gawler the Australian selectors voiced a mild interest in him and David for the 1982 World Championships.

Our personal problem enlarged. If I went to Australia I gave up a ten-year career. If David came to England, not only did he lose a secure job but now he would leave behind a good horse, too, and forsake another chance of representing his country.

For a month we hit a stalemate. The telephone bill continued to rise as we each sat through long periods of expensive silence unable to find a solution. Neither of us would allow the other to give up any of the things for which the other had worked.

Since his return to Brisbane David had saved what money he could by working at night in pubs as well as all day in photography. As Fair Deal was half owned by me, I sent over what money I could afford. In mid-July both Fair Deal and David made the long flight across the world. There was no other answer. After three and a half years of honourable service Charlie Micklem was leaving to lead a more independent life. There would at least therefore be a job for David, helping on our small farm and with the horses.

A few days after their arrival in July, Falmouth Bay gave me a much improved ride at Luhmühlen to finish ninth. He was still a long way from being top-class, but he was slowly closing the gap.

That summer was busy. I had seven horses to ride and all except one were of Advanced standard. It meant leaving my bed at 5 a.m. each morning, but it was worth it. The horses were going extremely well. I was in harmony with nearly all of them.

Both Beagle Bay and Mairangi won their Advanced classes at Dauntsey, the first important event of the summer season. At last Mairangi was feeling better. The well-known vet Geoffrey Brain had advised us to let him inhale the new medication 'Cromovet' for a few days each month. This treatment, combined with no hay for forty-eight hours before a competition, had produced the long-sought-after result. It seemed that his lungs had been over-stretched at Lexington and the scar tissue that gathered in consequence made them less able to expand. With clean airways and no bulk in the stomach for his lungs to push against, Mairangi sprang into a new, spirited life, three years after we had bought him.

85

Mairangi beginning to look happy and find his form again in the autumn of 1981. (*John Elliot*)

During the spring, at Badminton, Gossip had achieved his century. He came bottom in the dressage with 101.4 penalty points. Charlie, his rider, had taken a calculated gamble, suggested by a dressage expert, with the way in which Gossip was warmed up. Gossip would have none of it.

Possibly that last dreadful display of dressage took the pressure off me when I resumed riding him again in June 1981. I could not do any worse, so I relaxed and never came up against Gossip

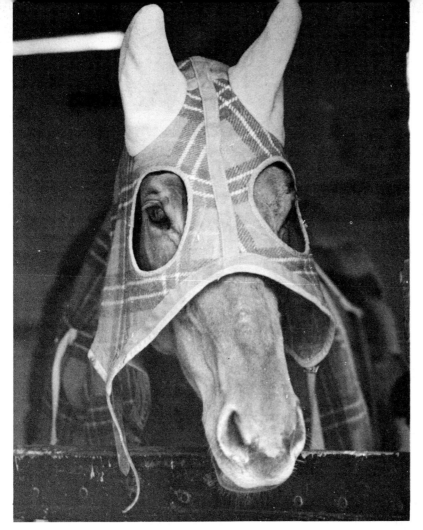

Fair Deal, David's young Australian horse, with whom he returned to England in July 1981. He wears an Australian hood with ears that we had specially made for him as he felt the cold of the English winters. (*David Green*)

or asked him for anything when schooling. In a matter of weeks his whole body visibly untensed when he realised there was nothing to fight and slowly he dared to take hold of the bit. The more he realised my hands were not going to move about, accidentally chopping him in the mouth as they asked for submission, the more confidence he developed. The passwords for this particular horse were never to ask; wait for him to give and then build quietly on that. Gradually it became clearer to me why, in 1977, when he had schooled Gossip in Germany, Herbert Rehbein had made the final accolade to my abilities as a dressage rider. He declared that if Gossip were bigger he would have him as his own dressage horse.

When Gossip gave, he gave his whole lovely, supple body. At thirteen he was too stiff to produce very good lateral work or any extended trot, but even without these movements he stunned judges everywhere he went into giving him good marks.

For five years he had suffered from his reputation stalking into the arena before he did, and in many tests he was marked possibly lower than he should have been. Now, he was benefiting from exactly the reverse. No one actually accused me, but there must have been some who were certain that I had found and administered an undetectable tranquilliser.

We set off for the One-Day Event Championships at Locko in high spirits. Foxy was there for a quiet school, and both Mairangi and Gossip had a chance of success. We felt luck was beginning to run our way. Maybe we should have curtailed our optimism when, on arrival at Locko, we discovered what Gossip had been

Despite being packed in an overnight bag, Lucky Teddy had his right eye chewed off by Gossip on the way up to Locko. (*David Green*)

David and I re-examine the Normandy Bank into water at Locko early in the competition. Already it had caused undue trouble and David Morton, course-builder, is also inspecting the bank for a cause. The minimal depth of sand on top of the platform of sleepers can be clearly seen to the right of the Midland Bank's griffin. (*Kit Houghton*)

doing during the journey. The rascal had managed to unzip my overnight bag, extricate my little five-inch lucky teddy and chew off one of his eyes.

The anticipated high changed suddenly to an impressive low after the cross-country. Compared to 1976 when Wide Awake died as he won Badminton and Be Fair suffered his Montreal injury, it was small-fry, but for a time I thought it was a repeat. I feared that Gossip had broken a bone behind his knee and Mairangi had crippled his hitherto trouble-free back.

Sitting well back neither Gossip nor I seem to be in too much trouble but his sharp little hooves had found a way through the thin layer of sand on the take-off platform. Consequently he skidded across its top and his vital point of balance was tipped too far forwards. He crumpled on landing. (*Press Association*)

Ducked. (*Press Association*)

Poor, poor Gossip, as bold and brave as always. He attacked the Normandy Bank into water with infinitely more care and less speed than he would have done three years earlier. Although the three-inch layer of sand on the take-off platform was enough for some to take a grip, for Gossip it was not. Those sharp little hooves went straight through the sand and onto the naked wet boards beneath. He skidded across the top of the raised jetty and plummetted into the river six feet below him. There, he was met by an unforgivable layer of sharp-edged stones which ripped slices of flesh from the front of both of the gums of his mouth and his knees and from the extremities of several other horses besides.

Once my bearings and breath had recovered from this ducking I was able to enjoy the amusing side of the situation. After all, falling into the water is the original joke.

But the smile was wiped from my face in a matter of seconds. I realised that the indestructible little tyrant who had shared my life and many of my nightmares and dreams for the past six years, was badly hurt.

Angela Tucker's Willow Pattern sustained identical injuries to Gossip's. Through its bad construction, many other horses fell at this fence. It became the bogey fence of the course and on account of it the Championships suffered much abuse. The fence was dismantled before the following year.

Mairangi pulled up very lame behind, after galloping round the cross-country course with ease. A few hours later a telephone call came through from home to say that Beagle Bay had an enormous front leg below the knee.

Ginny Holgate's victory, along with Mike Tucker's in the Novice Championships, were two of the happy parts of Locko. They are both people who carry the true spirit of eventing on their backs. Their positive attitudes of quiet determination and lack of jealousy, are their hall-marks. For the last decade both of them had struggled to overcome some devastating doses of misfortune whilst I had enjoyed equally devastating doses of the opposite.

Watching Gossip unable to turn in his stable except by rearing around his hind legs, seeing Mairangi with one hind leg held off the ground, knowing that the rising star we had left behind was injured too, made me ask again why I enjoyed eventing.

If it was all about winning then probably I would not enjoy it. Luckily, for us at home, it is about building partnerships with animals. It is about them finding themselves and the rider finding himself, through the mutual trust and confidence they develop in each other. That is why we love it and that is why it hurts when they are hurt.

Twenty-four hours later the world was already a happier place at Appleshaw. We drank to Gossip as he returned from a visit to the X-ray machine with clean plates and already in much less discomfort. Mairangi's lameness behind was looking less and less serious. It seemed he had an acutely twisted ankle. And Beagle Bay's leg had been stung by a bee, bitten by a rat or a snake, or possibly a blackthorn had lost itself inside his flesh.

After eight consecutive years in the British team I was dropped for the 1981 European Championships in Denmark, which took place two weeks after Locko. Out of all the horses in our yard, there was not one that was either of sufficient standard or sound enough to go. In six years Gossip had never had one day off because of lameness; I had been relying on him for Denmark. Jo reminded me of our conversation ten months earlier after she had returned to us at Appleshaw, when I had said that we must not be downhearted if, after our reorganisation, 1981 did not immediately go well.

Disappointment was soon quenched. The week before Locko in mid-August, Regal Realm had taken me to our first combined event at Billesdon. He had shown me his very special talents and now at least I had the time to start taking him seriously and working him daily myself.

After several tough battles during the spring, Charlie had settled Poncho in his canter work at home. Provided the rider kept perfectly still he would remain in the required pace. The tiniest movement from on top would fire him off like a rocket. This horse was going to continue teaching me where Gossip left off – sitting very still has never been one of my strengths, be it on a horse or on a chair.

Before our first event Regal Realm and I had not done much together. A few canters on the hills had indicated the difficulties and a short cross-country practice had sharpened us up. In the spring it had become clear that there was a refusal in Poncho. Among a few others he had produced a defiant and last-second stop at a coffin, a fence followed a few yards later by a ditch. In late July I took him back to that same coffin. He did it again. I beat him fairly hard several times. The way he had stopped was dirty and it was imperative that right from the start of our partnership he should know that there was only one thing that was forbidden. Some refusals occur because the horse genuinely does not understand or because something happens beyond his control such as skidding into a fence. On these occasions I will not punish my horse. He will probably still receive one slap because he must learn that, for whatever reason, it is wrong to stop until he has reached the other side of the obstacle. 'Spare the rod and spoil the child';

once a horse has learned that he can be disobedient, it is extremely difficult to cure him.

Regal Realm's intelligence and his sensitivity are highly developed. For the duration of the events in this book he never again had to be reprimanded.

His dressage mark was near the bottom in Billesdon's Open Intermediate class. Unlike Gossip he appeared to have a calmer attitude but any attempt to take a contact with his mouth, no matter how gentle, had the effect of making him raise his head and slow down. He seemed dead to both my legs and would almost disappear backwards between them as he withdrew under me. Possibly his reluctance to take hold of the bit derived from vivid memories of losing his eye-tooth in his early days as a stock horse.

The pouring rain on the baked clay ground did not hinder his cross-country round. Repeated attempts to slow him down received the minimum of attention. In preference to a prolonged fight such as he and Charlie had endured at their last competition at Tidworth in May, I let him go at his own pace.

Hurtling through the country, he reminded me of Village Gossip as he scampered across ridge and furrow, exploding over each fence like a squib. Here, dared I think, was the horse that I never believed could exist? He seemed to have all the dramatic qualities which are Gossip's, but he possessed a scopier jump and a more settled temperament.

Every day we worked at our dressage. All I could hope to do was encourage him to stretch out his concertina neck and look for the bit whilst maintaining his forward momentum. Soon I stopped working him in the outdoor school and chose different fields. He would switch off too quickly in the fenced arena and begin to retract and slow down almost before he had started.

Early in the year Charlie and Poncho had a little help with their dressage from David Hunt. Soon we agreed that Poncho was not yet in a position to be worthy of such lessons. 'If you ever want

---

Regal Realm is such a sharp and athletic jumper that I have always found it difficult to keep with him over a fence. In this picture we are jumping at home. Although the fence is barely two feet high, I have been thrown to the left and am struggling to regain a central balance. (*Stuart Newsham*)

to be a World Champion, you had better stop buying horses that can't move,' was the extent of the comment David passed on Poncho. On the whole, the standard in the sport is now too high to be able to succeed without a good performance on the first day.

At Crondall Open Intermediate, our next event, his test had improved by ten marks. Without trying he produced the second fastest cross-country round and finished fourth, one placing better than at Billesdon.

His fighting across country was much reduced by exchanging the nutcracker action of the snaffle for a straight-bar vulcanite bit, worn with a cross noseband.

A month after our first competition together Poncho produced a dressage test as opposed to a series of irregular squiggles. He tied with Clarissa Strachan on Delphy Kingfisher after the FEI test had been completed in our first Advanced event.

The cross-country at Powderham was one of the most difficult one-day event courses I have met. Regal Realm never flinched. He was relegated to second by virtue of Kingfisher's slightly faster time.

Three days earlier we had experimented by having our first dressage lesson together. Suddenly he seemed to click both mentally and physically and things began to fall into place. From then until the end of the season he continued to make steady and determined progress. The more he comprehended the more he tried.

Schooling at home. With his over-developed under-neck muscle we both found it hard to do any work. His whole outline is hollow and resisting the bit and contact. (*Stuart Newsham*)

September was hectically busy. No sooner had we returned with five horses from Powderham than it was time to leave at 6 a.m. for Burghley with Beagle Bay and Gossip, the latter apparently recovered from his Locko injury.

At exactly 6 a.m. the telephone went in my cottage at Appleshaw – I had completely overslept. Jo had done everything and the horses were ready to leave. By 6.25 we were rolling on our four-and-a-half-hour journey north.

We were within half an hour of our destination when Jo enquired if I had remembered the horses' passports. I had not. Such is the strict ruling in international competition now that our horses were only allowed to off-load at Burghley if they stayed in the quarantine stables, well apart from everyone else's, until their passports had been produced.

Poor David had to leap into the car at home and bring up the passports before the horses could be officially eliminated at 3 p.m.

Later in the afternoon Gossip failed the preliminary vet's inspection and was eliminated from the competition. Only those to whom it has happened would know what a ghastly feeling this produces. If you know your business, you do not produce a horse at the first inspection if he is not going to pass.

Since Gossip's apparent recovery, he had worked, galloped and jumped and been test-trotted daily up the gravel drive with no unsoundness noticeable. Therein lies the lesson I learned: gravel and tarmac are two entirely different surfaces concerning the amount of concussion each produces. Gossip may have been sound on the gravel but on the tarmac at the vetting he was not. We assumed that there was still deep bruising behind his knee from his fall at Locko and that this was brought to light only on completely unforgiving ground.

Later that night we had just settled down to sleep in the horse-box when some friends shouted across the darkened lorry park. 'Come quickly, Beagle Bay has kicked through his stable wall.'

There, standing with his hindleg in the air, was the one remaining hope. Beagle Bay had kicked a huge hole in the flimsy wall of his temporary stabling. As we bandaged him up, I cursed myself again for not bothering to produce a fit and sound Mairangi Bay at the vet's inspection. So certain was I that both Gossip and Beagle Bay were all right that I had left Mairangi at home, and now it seemed as if neither of the other two could run.

Thankfully the only effect this midnight frolic had on Beagle Bay's condition was to enable him to be rehoused in one of the few permanent stone-walled stables.

He gave a very satisfactory showing in the dressage although he ended the day in only thirteenth place. It did not unduly surprise me to find ourselves so comparatively low down the list after a good test, luck simply was not with us.

At the last fence on the steeplechase course the following day there was a decisive change in our fortunes. Beagle Bay stood off so far that he could barely reach the fence itself. I was catapulted up his neck as he landed. Somehow whilst struggling to regain his own balance Beagle Bay kept his neck up and put me back in the saddle. If a horse does something like that for you when he could so easily have done the opposite, you are inclined to take on a new dimension of respect and affection for him. I think this helped us greatly in what was to come.

The cross-country seemed a well-built, reasonably easy course. In fact it rode a well-built and surprisingly difficult one.

Beagle Bay had done only two Advanced and three Open Inter-mediate classes with me, before which he ran in junior one- and three-day events with his previous owner. He was therefore still an inexperienced horse although he was eleven years old.

He had courage and pride, and he jumped on and on, trying to sort out the problems as best he could. He jumped into the Trout Hatchery unhesitatingly and crumpled on landing – his head went under the water, yet somehow this time I did not nearly fall off him. He had water in his ears after his involuntary submersion, about which he was most indignant, and thereafter he ignored most of my directions.

99

Near the end of the course something happened that had never befallen me before. I could not attract his attention in order to tell him that I wanted to slow down and turn off the homeward track to jump a fence. Eventually I was forced to give an immense haul on one rein. He changed tactics and answered it so quickly, politely bringing his head round to my call, that he threw me completely off balance. I knew that I had gone past the point of no return, and all I could do was try to slow him up enough to fall off and not lose my horse before we entered the penalty zone of the next fence. There followed a nightmare few moments with him zigging while I zagged, until he eventually came to a halt. I was able to readjust my balance without actually touching down on the ground, and we continued on our way.

In a hurry to make up the time I had lost doing unnecessary acrobatics, I then over-angled the penultimate fence which Beagle Bay hit so hard with the sides of his off-fore and hindlegs that he nearly came down.

It was this error that had Jo, her brother William, David, myself and Terry Walsh from OCL, up till late that night. Beagle Bay was in the lead at the end of the cross-country day so we had to do what we could to try and make him sound for the final test, the show-jumping the following day. Hot and then cold compresses were alternated on the sizable and painful bruise that had appeared on the outside of his off-fore ankle. It was so sore that we wondered how he would ever manage to walk on it, let alone trot or jump.

As a last resort I telephoned a spiritual healer and explained Beagle Bay's problem. I was told to be in his stable at ten o'clock that night and encircle the offending joint, without actually touching it, with my forefingers and thumbs.

On the stroke of ten I was kneeling at my grey horse's feet, fingers and thumbs in place. All five of us were in the stable in complete silence concentrating the power of our positive thought. During those same five minutes the healer was doing likewise.

I do believe in miracles and, with a great deal of help from on high, and none from pain-killing drugs, because their use is so strictly controlled nowadays, he trotted out sound at the vet's inspection the next morning.

He jumped an impeccable and happy clear round in the show-

Beagle Bay wins Burghley, 1981. Terry Walsh, OCL's Head of PR, receives the Raleigh Trophy. (*Findlay Davidson*)

jumping, giving inches to spare over each fence, and won for himself the Raleigh Trophy.

After the various traumas we had endured throughout Burghley it was a most unexpected outcome. It was OCL's first major win with a horse of their ownership in their four years of sponsorship. How they deserved this reward. Never, through all the gloomiest of periods, had they put any pressure on me to do well, but they must have thought that my successes were a thing of the past. Certainly I was beginning to believe that never again could I win a three-day event.

Psychologically, it was probably the most important moment since Burghley 1977. How grateful and thrilled we all were. Not least the ex-owners, the Naylor-Leylands, who had educated Beagle Bay between the ages of four and nine.

Six days later Regal Realm galloped his way through some of the nastiest horizontal rain I have ever ridden in, to second place in the Advanced class at Tetbury Horse Trials. Within twelve hours David, Joanna and I abandoned Appleshaw for yet another week, leaving behind piles of muddy tack and horses for those unfortunates remaining in the yard. We were destined to fly to Washington for the United States Open Championships at Chesterlands, Pennsylvania. We arose early and checked that all the horses were sound and undamaged, before we set off for Heathrow.

The British competitors were not joined by their horses for a further two days as the latter had to be kept in quarantine in New York and no one was allowed in with them. It was less than appealing to have to change the horses' diet and care completely, only five days before an international competition. Nothing could be done about it and to our surprise none of them suffered.

Foxy was the lucky one chosen for the trip and he took a serious step forward in his career. His dressage test was much more relaxed and controlled. It was because of David Hunt's advice with Foxy that I began to understand a little more about the subtleties of riding a horse off the contact. He had worked very hard to help me with this horse and eventually it was beginning to pay dividends.

Falmouth Bay completed the cross-country fast and clear to give me the least scaring round I had enjoyed with him. He was third in the US Open Championships behind Bruce Davidson on

The win that decided our marriage. Burghley, 1981.

the seven-year-old J.J. Babu and Karen Stives on Silent Partner. He was, at last, looking like a top-class horse. Our tough programme for him, including three three-day events in four months, had worked, or nearly. A week later it became evident that he had strained a tendon. It would be a year before he could do his next three-day event. We would be back to where we started in his education. These then are some of the risks and disappointments involved in trying to find and mould top-class horses.

OPPOSITE and ABOVE: Falmouth Bay excels himself in America, taking third place in the US Championships, Chesterlands, September 1981.

The night the American event finished, David, my mother and I flew back to London. Within three days the Wylye Three-Day Event was upon us. David hoped to ride Major Lycett's Chili Con Carne there and I had a Novice in the two-day event.

David's luck was still out. Fair Deal had only recently recovered from a ripped shoulder where a horse had kicked him in the ten-acre field that was the collecting-ring at his first English event. On our return we found that Chili Con Carne was not fit for Wylye. He had scraped his leg on a dressage board a little while earlier and the bruising was still apparent.

As if that was not enough, no sooner had Swift Deal recovered from the trouble which kept him out of action in 1980 than he developed chronic and fast-deteriorating navicular, a type of arthritis of the foot bone. By September 1981 he was sore merely walking around in his field. David was faced with the same heart-stretching decision as I had been over Be Fair.

There was one whole week at home between Wylye and setting out for the final assault of the year, Boekelo, the Dutch International Championships.

It was at the end of this week, after David and my family at last found time to talk, that we announced our engagement.

No one knew at the time, but some weeks before Burghley when David and I were discussing marriage possibilities and were unable to come to any firm decision, we eventually agreed that I would marry him if I won Burghley. It was a facetious way of not committing myself. Having been single for twenty-seven years and become not a little sceptical about the success of the state of marriage, I was as frightened as anyone of making a mistake.

Superstitions play a large part in my life and when to my amazement Beagle Bay won Burghley, there was no looking back.

Simon and my mother were wonderful. They performed their duty by putting us both through interrogation to ensure that we knew what we were doing and then supported us with everything they had all the way to the altar.

We take the plunge. A beautiful diamond and sapphire ring becomes mine. (*Daily Telegraph*)

There were plenty of raised eyebrows and poor David had to suffer the effects of some British snobbery. He was very handsome, only twenty-one, he had no proper job in England and no riches in Australia. He was quiet and shy on first acquaintance and therefore people could be forgiven for thinking rude thoughts about both of us.

Regal Realm competed under the OCL flag, not because they had relieved me of my painful investment, but because we felt it gave my noble sponsors one more exhibition-piece.

A year had elapsed since Regal Realm first came to Appleshaw; I had been riding him for a quarter of that time. He was changing. His body had built up and his neck looked stronger. His eye had softened and widened as, month by month, he allowed himself increasingly to enjoy the beginnings of human affection.

By the end of the season I was aware of a considerable change in him. He would now let me hug him and actually begin to give something in return instead of sharply pulling away his head the moment he felt cornered. It dawned on me then, that Jo was becoming very attached to him. She has her favourites amongst the horses but none of them have enjoyed quite the extent of the worship that she gave to Be Fair. Over the following year Poncho took Be Fair's place and revelled in the consequences as his self-confidence developed.

He was always a little tetchy about being girthed up, but while his self-assurance increased, so, it seemed, did his sensitivity. As his girths were tightened, his head would begin to whirl round in fast circles on the end of a neck that shook up and down; he would lay his ears flat back and bite repeatedly at the air. Underneath he is a sweet, kind, patient horse; such antics therefore appear quite out of character. Oddly he also found it difficult to become accustomed to sudden noise, a trait which he has carried from birth. He flinches at the slightest unexpected sound. X-raying him is nearly impossible: every time the operating button, which makes a soft burr, is pressed, he jumps and ruins the picture. Whenever Jo dresses him in a freshly laundered summer sheet he arches his neck high, snorting vigorously at the new smell and sound of starched cotton.

Poncho and Mairangi were destined for Boekelo. In the habitual

Kangaroo-like, Regal Realm pinged around the solid fences of Boekelo. (*Findlay Davidson*)

drizzly weather of the lowlands of Holland in late autumn, Mairangi actually enjoyed his first three-day event in three years. He produced his best dressage test and a happy, interested clear round across country. Purposely I did not push him and he finished in eighth place.

Regal Realm, it transpired, was everything I had hardly dared hope he could be. He tried so hard in his dressage and was only two marks behind Mairangi. He tore around the cross-country course springing, kangaroo-style, over anything in his path. Like so many horses from Down Under, he does not bother to drop his head and arch his back over a jump, he simply pings from the take-off ground like a gymnast springing off the board in front of a wooden horse. Poncho relishes the feeling of his power and he becomes sour if he does not jump regularly, yet he rarely has his ears pricked over a fence. Threequarters of the way around Boekelo we very, very nearly fell apart. Jumping neatly down the six-foot drop off a Normandy Bank, Poncho landed easily and took two strides of canter, after which all motion ceased. According to an experienced onlooker he tripped because he stood on his own over-reach boot. Momentarily he went down on his knees and nose and hastily ejected me to the end of his short neck. I was hanging there with my head looking down his forehead from between his ears for only a fraction of a second, but such catastrophic moments freeze as if caught in slow-motion.

Poncho threw up his head, as he adroitly corrected his own balance, thereby pushing me back down his neck. Instantly he took off at an unsettled gallop with the reins over his head and his jockey bouncing about on his withers in front of the saddle. Pushing myself back into the seat, I realised that although I still had hold of the end of the reins, they were both on the same side of his neck. Somehow he had to be slowed down for he was closing inordinately quickly on a vertical bank with a boggy ditch in front of it. In full gallop I leant down to one side over his narrow shoulder and with both arms under his neck, cast the loop of the reins upwards. The second attempt worked and his head went through the loop. I was able to sit up and pull him back just in time before he cartwheeled up the bank. Luck played a strong hand in Regal Realm's second place to Fiona Moore's Squire's Holt as the final international event of 1981 drew to a close.

In 1977 George won Burghley, Killaire was third in the USA and Gossip was second in Boekelo. How strange that four years later, although with different horses, the same pattern emerged. Remembering what had befallen us at the World Championships the following year, 1978 at Lexington, I prayed the pattern would not repeat itself in 1982.

Immediately after the cross-country at Boekelo I decided that I would burn all our over-reach boots. For years I had been waiting for an incident like that to persuade me to have the courage of my convictions. It had never seemed possible that the rubber, bell-shaped boots worn loosely under the front fetlock joints could be strong enough to prevent injury from an over-reach. If they were, then they would have to be made of extra thick rubber, which the horse would find too heavy to wear. Now that they had been responsible for very nearly uprooting Poncho, I did not feel foolhardy in evicting them.

In a state of great delight with our new star that had begun to twinkle so brightly, we arrived home from Holland in the horsebox via the North Sea ferry.

Within forty-eight hours Poncho had contracted a virus. He stood miserably in his stable with his head and ears drooping, shivering and tense. He had a temperature of 104°F.

Two days later he was fighting for his life. On the fourth consecutive day that Paul, our vet, came to see him, he admitted he was very worried. Not an alarmist, Paul nonetheless could not understand why Poncho's blood-test read normal nor why he did not respond to any of the antibiotics or calcium injections he was given. On the contrary his discomfort appeared to be increasing and his tummy sounded dreadful through the stethoscope.

For four days he had not eaten. Jo spent hours with him till late each night, trying to persuade him to take a little honey or a few shoots of green grass or sprigs of hay. Once we gave each other a proper fright when we collided at midnight in the kitchen-garden. Each of us carried a bucket which we were filling with the fresh grass we had picked and neither of us knew that the other had left her bed.

On that fourth day Paul threw new light on the dilemma and wondered whether Poncho had contracted a straightforward travel virus and on account of this felt too ill to walk about. Being very fit and having just finished the exertions of a three-day event, this immobility could consequently have compacted his insides. Paul tubed him with two gallons of saline mixture and in so doing he saved his life, for that afternoon proved to be the turning point in Poncho's illness.

In the few days that he was sick Poncho lost two hundredweight of condition, which took him eight months to replace.

In early November we sent out the invitations to our wedding. December 4th had been elected as the date and we would be married at Wilton. Through the kindness of my cousin, Henry Herbert, we were able to hold the reception in one of the most

111

beautiful rooms in Europe: the seventeenth-century, Inigo Jones 'Double Cube', the *pièce de résistance* of Wilton House.

At seventy-eight years old, Nanny gamely and enthusiastically agreed to spend a month at Appleshaw to make my wedding dress. During my childhood she had made most of my clothes and ever since I was young I had always wanted her to make my wedding dress. Even if I married a millionaire a dress made by Nanny would outvalue any by the world's top couturiers.

Nanny and I designed it together after my mother and I spent two days looking for suitable material. Until then I had never appreciated how many different shades of white there were.

Single-handed my mother organised the wedding and reception inside six weeks. The flair and taste she imparted and the manner in which she categorically left no corner unturned was a revelation.

Karol, my half-sister, who has been an enthusiastic supporter of all my horse pursuits since they began, lent me her lovely thirteen-year-old daughter, Lorna, for our bridesmaid. Knicker-bockers were the height of fashion and I planned a pair for her in lemon-yellow silk, with which she wore a high open-necked

Nanny zips me into the finished article. (*Henry Herbert*)

My brother, Simon, who gave me away, and Lorna Maxwell, my neice, as bridesmaid. Oliver Plum was never far away. (*Akhtar Hussein*)

white shirt and white tights. David saw some of the yellow material and with badly disguised despair asked if I did not think it was going a little too far having my wedding dress in my cross-country colours? Telling him I felt it was very appropriate, we led him on to believe the fallacy. My idea was that he would be so relieved when I joined him at the altar to find I was in white, that he would relax a little. As it turned out he was too nervous to notice.

Yellow seems to have played an important part in my life. At a very young age, when I was still struggling to learn how to read, I remember distinctly lying in bed one morning looking at a picture and word book called *The Little Yellow Duck*. Suddenly the letters

The reception at Wilton House. (*Akhtar Hussein*)

in the word 'yellow' formed a sound in my mouth and from that day I could read.

December 4th began a grey, dull day, but a day that I enjoyed probably more than any other in my life. As my brother Simon and I entered the church the clouds had folded away. Inside, shining through the huge circular stained-glass window high above the altar, sunbeams intensified on the aisle. It was a radiantly happy day for us. Only twice before can I remember having cheek-ache from smiling too widely for too long.

That night we wasted British Airways' generously donated first-class seats by sleeping for nearly all of the nine-hour flight to Nairobi.

We relished a five-week honeymoon, interrupted by a week's teaching on a British Airways' clinic in return for our air-fares. During the teaching clinic someone told me they had overheard another saying how sad they thought it was that I was an alcoholic. Such a story stole the prize for the best rumour to date. All my life I have disliked alcohol and never drunk it.

In between searching for lion and elephant and watching them in their natural state, I wrote thank-you letters for wedding presents to over two hundred people. We were staggered at the repeated open-handedness of friends and relatives both close and distant.

During a holiday I try to banish all thoughts of horses from my mind, in order to return thoroughly refreshed for the oncoming year. Nevertheless I could not help a backward glance at Regal Realm and the promise he undoubtedly held for the future. There was no doubt that I owed Australia a large debt of gratitude. She was occupying my father on business in 1968 when my mother and I bought Be Fair. He had long since forgotten the little we both knew about horses and if he had not been abroad at the time, he would never have let us buy him. Australia had also given me a very special husband thirteen years later, as well as a horse who could possibly one day prove to be unique.

For some inexplicable reason Regal Realm's dressage became slowly worse during the spring of 1982. Possibly I did not build him up again sufficiently steadily or with enough feeling for his weaknesses. Very often a horse has to go through a bad stage before he improves, but this bad stage went on too long. Something in the way I was riding him aggravated him; he would not settle onto the contact or soften his back. By Crookham, our first event of the 1982 season, he had reverted to feeling like a glass horse; if I moved, he would crack. He wiggled his way down the long sides of the arena and never felt submissive or balanced enough to square the corners. One day I schooled him in a jumping saddle and he seemed to soften more easily under this. He had lost so much muscle during his post-Boekelo illness that possibly he was no longer strong enough to take the more centralised, defined weight of a dressage saddle. Consequently throughout the spring, in both practice and competitions, I continued to ride him in a lightweight jumping saddle.

However, there was nothing about either his jumping or his galloping that suggested he was any weaker than the previous year.

Brake problems returned. He had become increasingly strong towards the end of the previous autumn, so much so that I dared not ride him at Boekelo in the gentle straight-bar vulcanite bit. Replacing this with an eggbutt helped for threequarters of the course. Following the upset he suffered when tripping as he stepped on his over-reach boot, I had minimal further control as he motor-biked and skidded around the twisty woodland paths. Eventually he came up against the penultimate fence with his ears precariously near my teeth as he stared at the grey skies above him. He almost refused when he put his head down and saw a murky ditch full of water four yards beyond the rails. Maybe he remembered the punishment he received for refusing at a similar fence two months earlier, for somehow he spilt himself, in a series of uneven spurts, over the rails and across the stream.

Much of his pulling was as a result of his sensitivity. He was still very shy about his head. Putting on his bridle or halter had to be executed quietly and slowly. Tightening the lower strap of his cross noseband was never an easy task either. I was never sure if this was because of painful memories of his early days or because he hated to have his whiskers pulled.

Before the spring season began I took him to Wylye for two practice sessions. Over one hundred and fifty obstacles, designed and built by Lord and Lady Hugh Russell, space themselves across hundreds of acres of Wiltshire downland. It is probably the world's finest cross-country training centre and in Rosemary Russell it certainly has one of the most skilled instructors of cross-country

Lord and Lady Hugh Russell with Dick Stillwell (right). Despite her crippling accident nearly twenty years ago, Lady Hugh and her husband lead an extremely busy life almost entirely devoted to the cause of helping British eventing. (*Stuart Newsham*)

riding. Since I was fourteen she has persistently given me the benefit of her advice. I owe much of the confidence and tactics of my riding across country to her understanding and to her tireless, and sometimes tough, teaching.

She had watched Poncho in Holland so I discussed the control problem with her. She wondered if maybe he was fighting the restrictions of the martingale. I therefore slackened its tension. His bit was changed to a French-link, a double-jointed snaffle, to see if he was more comfortable in that. He seemed to be, but the basic secret of his control lay in balancing him in front of the fence much earlier than a normal horse and, as usual, much of the success depended on how still I could sit. Once upset by such a happening as that in Holland, he was gone.

The end of that winter and the early spring of 1982 were cold and savage. Heavy snow over a prolonged period, followed by intense cold, had finally ruined our outdoor manége and rendered it unrideable. We schooled in jagged circles in different parts of a field each day. Despite these inconveniences, those normally heavy months passed lightly for me. David and I lived, worked and breathed together. We were both intrigued by the same subject: the horse. Until then I had not registered what a comparatively lonely life eventing at world-class standard had been. I suppose life had never stopped still for long enough to notice it. Each and every day was busy and full.

Frequently I had to be away from home involved in unequine activities. There were a number of meetings in London to attend, including board meetings of the Devitt Insurance Brokers for whom I worked as counsel to the Devitt Equestrian Plan. The General Advisory Council of the BBC held a meeting each quarter and there were several duties concerning other subjects that could not be neglected. Often I would be required in a different part of the country to deliver a lecture-demonstration or take part in a quiz or chat show for TV, the latter always being tremendous fun.

At home if I was not riding, then I was telephoning, sorting out the entries, lessening a pile of desk work, or organising a programme so that Appleshaw stables continued to run when I was abroad competing. By evening, I rarely had enough energy to socialise and would fall into bed. Eight hours later I was either

'Lileric', our cottage – outside and inside. (*David Green*)

LEFT: 'Australia' -- the bathroom represents Down Under. (*David Green*)
RIGHT: David's sense of humour is reflected in this trophy which hangs in our living room. Instead of a fox's mask or a stag's head we have a kangaroo. (*David Green*)

schooling a horse or working one in his fitness routine on the hills. Decisions had to be taken and responsibilities borne every day of the week. My mother ran the house and was always wise if her advice was sought. Working with me was a loyal and conscientious team of girls in the stable and Judy, our part-time secretary in the office. Even so, in the final analysis, I was alone.

Suddenly, in 1982, there were two of us; the work did not halve but the fun more than doubled – the only threat to our marriage being that tedious but necessary invention, the telephone, which leaves David wondering if I married him or it.

Chili Con Carne had been on the market all winter and, as he

LEFT: Mr Cook, Appleshaw's 'Mr Everything'. Twenty years ago he tended our one-time dairy herd. Latterly, he has built stables and cross-country fences, and has looked after the encumbrances surrounding our stable and home life. (*David Green*) RIGHT: Tomato Stanley Green at three months old. (*Alison Hicks*)

was not sold, Major Lycett asked David to ride this huge three-quarter thoroughbred Irish hunter at Badminton. Chili was not unlike Killaire, except he was nearly twice the size. He was innately kind and honest and had a fascinating manner of landing over his jumps. He would unfold his legs earlier than other horses and put his front feet almost horizontally out in front of him as he crossed the top of the fence and began his downward descent. He looked a little like someone doing a racing dive. We loved this unique characteristic as much as we loved Chili, but we could not foresee that it would lead to his downfall.

For a time we could not decide who would ride what and

121

whether or not we would swop horses at intervals. Soon it became obvious that I would ride Poncho and either Beagle Bay or Gossip at Badminton and therefore David took over Mairangi. He struck up, remarkably quickly, a profound relationship with both him and Chili. It was quite clear that he genuinely loved his horses, an unusual characteristic to find in a man.

To seal our happiness we had adopted Tomato. There are only two families of Australian Cattle Dogs (or 'Heelers', as they are known) in England. Tomato did not possess the right blotches in the right places and was therefore the least expensive of a litter that was born in Dorset.

My Cavalier King Charles Spaniel, Oliver Plum, had long since been taken over by my mother. He had been my constant companion for nine years but once David came into my life Oliver loathed him and refused to have much more to do with me. Regrettably, he was also too much of a snob to enjoy life in a tiny cottage.

One evening that spring we had a call from Harold Lusk, the international horse dealer from Belfast for whom David had worked two years earlier. He told David that he knew of a really good event horse in Ireland and could produce an owner for it if I would agree to ride it. Apparently the prospective owner was already involved in show jumping, but wanted to buy and sponsor a top event horse as an advertisement for his company.

This was a new encounter, a somewhat back-to-front situation. Previously people already owned the horses they wanted me to ride. This present concept placed a big onus on me, my chief worry being that if I agreed to ride this horse, then the prospective owner would put down a large sum and buy it. What happened, if after a few weeks or months, I felt the horse was not top-class? The owner would lose most of his money and I would feel partially responsible for having agreed to ride it. It was tempting to forget the whole possibility.

Having voiced my fears, I did eventually agree to a meeting. It was arranged that the intended purchaser would come down and take David and me out to dinner.

On that particular evening David was ill. I found myself alone in a Rolls-Royce with five dark-suited strangers and one attractive girl, none of whom I remembered meeting previously. For a moment I feared the Mafia had come for me. However, we all survived the evening and it culminated in the agreement that I would take the horse on provided his owner, John Burbidge, understood that if he was not good enough I would send him back.

A week later a grey, Irish-bred 16.2 hh gelding wandered up the back drive. In the flesh he looked uninteresting. On paper his credentials were good. He had won £80 show jumping and was an Irish Intermediate eventer. Apparently he had fallen only once and that was into a sheepwash at his one and only three-day event, the Novice class at Punchestown. From reports, he was not proficient at dressage but very fast across country. When Shannagh was put to the test he was certainly no good at dressage but he could not gallop either. For a month I struggled with him; he tried hard and he certainly jumped very well, but there was no zest in him, no merriment; life seemed an effort for this seven-year-old. He was not responding to his feeding or his training and, all in all, he was a somewhat common lump of disappointment. I did not envisage him making a very exciting advertisement for John Burbidge's company. Maybe he should be returned.

At the end of four weeks David Hunt worked Shannagh for twenty minutes. Despite the pottery inelegant strides he felt that this horse could be trained to come up off his forehand, where he had hung heavily for seven years. He believed there was possibly enough movement concealed there to produce good dressage. I relied on the expert's judgment, because I could not see any decent paces whatsoever in the horse. I knew only that he had a marvellous temperament and was clever and scopey over a fence. When it became clear that he was highly anaemic and full of redworm, I decided to keep him for a little longer and see how he felt when his health improved. Little did we know at the time that the results of that laboured decision were to open the lock-gates on another entirely new chapter in our lives.

By the very manner in which David's riding had improved so dramatically in the year and a half that he had spent in Great Britain, I knew that he would one day be very good. How soon that day would come I had no way of knowing.

Frensham, the first major Advanced one-day event of the spring season, gave me a shrewd idea.

Regal Realm sped around in beautiful and safe style at the

habitual great speed that he had adopted over the past two years. Mairangi and David clocked nearly ten seconds faster. With the huge Irish hunter, Chili, he then finished on exactly the same time as my speed-merchant. Neither of these two horses were previously recognised for their nippiness across the country.

Beagle Bay responded to my urging in a much less novice manner than he had at Burghley and both he and Regal Realm won their sections of the Advanced event. If he had not knocked a show-jump down with both his horses, David would have been second in each section.

The following weekend at Rushall Mairangi was second. Village Gossip showed everyone that being fourteen was a baby's age when, after his best dressage test, he pipped Beagle Bay into first place through his superior speed across country.

There was no need for Regal Realm to do Rushall, he had proved himself ripe for Badminton at Frensham. The question was, which of the two that were fighting it out at Rushall should make up my second ride?

Both horses were making a very strong claim to running at Badminton. Gossip, at fourteen, was possibly coming to his peak, although I thought he had reached it three years ago, and should have been over the top now. Beagle Bay was twelve and in a similar situation. Neither had age on his side to be denied the ultimate opportunity. What a wonderful position to be in. What a difficult choice to make.

No one could help with that final decision. Ultimately it had to be mine. There were equal amounts of pros and cons concerning each horse.

As over eighty horses filtered past the panel at the first vet's inspection at Badminton on the Wednesday afternoon, I stood propped against a wall of the great house, turning the problem over and over in my mind.

I ran Gossip up for the vets and he let out a squeal of joy as he turned to trot past them. I knew that I should give Beagle Bay the chance – although untried, I felt he was ready to meet the very considerable challenge that Badminton presented. But Gossip was ready too and he was in such high spirits.

That familar lump was sitting high in my throat as I made the declaration that Village Gossip would not run. He had done so much for me that horse, twice pulling me out of a psychological furrow of despondency, once at Badminton in 1978 and again at Fontainebleau in 1980. And now I was taking away from him his last great moment, Badminton.

After a while the magnitude of the contest itself lured my thoughts away from Gossip and his disappointment and by Friday night both David and I were as satisfied as ever we could be that all was ready for the big day.

Preparing and running four horses across country at Badminton takes some organising. Jo had written out the plan of attack that she and her tribe were going to follow. Everyone knew what they were going to do, and none better than the horses themselves who became very quiet and still on Friday night and Saturday morning.

The course was thoroughly walked. The general feeling was that it was tough, with no let-ups and too many drops, but the going was perfect and very fast.

Apart from Beagle Bay who suffered the inevitable 'luck of the draw' mark by going first, our dressage scores came out much

---

Chili Con Carne and David extend across the dressage arena. Badminton, 1982.

ABOVE: Regal Realm attempting his dressage test, Badminton, 1982. This performance left him in thirty-first position. He had reverted to the hollow outline with the bulging under-neck muscle. During that spring I rode him in a jumping saddle – a dressage saddle seemed to make him even more tense. (*Stuart Newsham*)

OPPOSITE: Mairangi and David soar over Fence 17. This obstacle was an unfinished bridge copied from a Danish innovation first seen at the European Championships in Horsens the previous autumn. (*Hugo Czerny*)

---

as we had expected. David rode Chili into tenth place on 52.2, deservedly the highest of our four and 6.8 points ahead of his other ride, Mairangi.

With our comparatively poor dressage marks and with the fast going across country, we knew our chances of victory were nil. However, the unattractive prospect of being the first to challenge that inhibiting course magnetised all my thoughts.

We could not have been more delighted with how well, bravely and honestly all our horses performed. The thrill of four such rounds was marred only by Major Lycett's poor Chili receiving a thoroughly unjust reward for his tremendous effort. His flamboyant straight-armed jumping style, coupled with his large weight landing over an excessive amount of drop fences – an ugly feature of

After months of hard preparation Joanna (right) waits in the Box at Badminton to tend to her charges as they finish Phase C. A ten-minute break is allowed each horse before commencing the cross-country. During that time the horse can be washed down, his boots, bandages and tack checked for security. The spare saddle, bridle and boots can be seen around the trunk. In the foreground is a tub of Vaseline and a rubber glove. The fronts of all four of the horse's legs are liberally greased to help him to slide out of difficulty if in trouble. (*Stuart Newsham*)

recent Badmintons – left him with a ruptured suspensory ligament.

Apart from having a new rider and one from his own latitude, Mairangi's fast clear was aided by his having spent the previous winter as Master's horse in Leicestershire with Joss Hanbury and by the Cromovet inhalations for his wind. David thus enjoyed his trip round Badminton and his first Whitbread horse, a small silver trophy presented to each of the first twelve riders. They were clear all the way through and finished in sixth place after the show jumping. Seventh was Regal Realm, who effected the fastest cross-country round out of all the starters, being forty-five seconds inside the time, and eighth was Beagle Bay.

The news of Poncho's jet-propelled circuit of Badminton soon reached Merv Bennett in Australia. He could not comprehend it.

ABOVE: Poncho approached the Lake fence at Badminton with his head held so high – as he fought my efforts to control him – that he barely saw the upturned boat that he was supposed to jump. He very nearly refused but somehow just managed to twist himself over. April 1982. (*Colorsport*) BELOW LEFT: Landing in the lake. For a nasty unbalanced second I feared we would be submerged (*Mike Roberts*) BELOW RIGHT: Relief – we are still afloat and together, although minus a stirrup. (*Mike Roberts*)

OPPOSITE ABOVE: Poncho jumped so big up the step out of the lake that he landed at the base of the ensuing rails and had to spring vertically into the air to avoid somersaulting over them. (*Mike Roberts*) OPPOSITE BELOW: We have little enough control three fences later at the Ski Jump ... (*Stuart Newsham*) THIS PAGE: ... Followed three strides later by a narrow set of rails at the head of a 'funnel'. (*Stuart Newsham*)

OCL were due to withdraw their sponsorship at the end of the year. After Badminton and with the MacConnal-Mason Gallery offering the bounty of half the sponsorship that we needed, we hoped that they might think again. They did, but with a new chairman and a drop in profits they felt they must terminate our association as planned.

Our whole sport was being re-structured in 1982. Owing to the Midland Bank's magnanimity, and the secure roots which it had provided, the sport had exploded in popularity during the past five years. By 1983 the Bank's thirteen-year blanket sponsorship of nearly all the important one-day events in the country as well

131

Beagle Bay shows how the lake fence should be tackled.

Badminton, 1982. (*Stuart Newsham*)

John Burbidge's Shannagh, competing at Sherborne Intermediate One-Day Event, May, 1982. He had a scopy and careful jump but completely lacked the zest and love of life necessary in a top-class horse. Would he ever make a very exciting advertisement for his owner's company? (*Kit Houghton*)

as some three-day events, was due to end. At home we felt this was a healthy prospect. Although at first it would be a struggle and its support would be widely missed, the withdrawal of the Midland Bank had the effect of opening up the sport and involving a great many more sponsors. Eventually this should lead to a greater amount of prize money and other opportunities for competitors to regain a more substantial proportion of the big sums of money laid out in maintaining a competition horse. As we were about to find further proof for ourselves, individual sponsorship was virtually unobtainable. There had to be other ways, therefore, of oiling the wheels.

Despite our strong support of the move to open up the sport, we were in effect cutting off our own water supply. Simon, David and I spent the first eight months of 1982 writing to, visiting and telephoning endless companies, advertising agents and public relations bodies in a search for personal sponsorship. We found that many of those who were even slightly connected with the equine market had already channelled their interest into sponsoring a competition. Logically this was how it should be. It is no use having competitors sponsored if competitions do not exist in which they can compete.

By the end of spring David and I had to begin to entertain the possibility that we might fail in our search for further sponsorship. Neither of us felt that we wanted to stay in England and compete on the occasional chance-ride that came our way. That would not be progress. Either we devoted our lives to competitive riding and did it properly, or, if that became an impossibility, we moved to Australia and started a completely different way of life.

One evening in May we were having a dinner party in our cottage, when David suddenly noticed that our five-month-old Tomato was missing. Most of that night we searched for him in vain. In the morning we looked in roadside ditches and under bridges. We feared he may have been run over, or possibly stolen. We searched endlessly, preferring, we decided, to discover him dead than not at all and never know what dreadful fate had befallen him.

At lunchtime our Australian working-pupil, Helen Carr, found him. He was alive. He must have been hit on the road the evening before and run in panic for nearly half a mile across the fields until his broken thigh-bone gave out and he collapsed. Helen found him lying on his side under a fence on the boundary between our land and our neighbour's. Had he gone in virtually any other direction, he would have run off our small acreage and we would never have seen him again.

Shortly after this unwelcome incident in mid-May, David with Botany Bay and myself with Gossip went over to Ireland for the Punchestown International Three-Day Event.

Six weeks earlier when both Might Tango and Gossip had to be withdrawn from Badminton I had a joke bet with Bruce Davidson, Tango's rider. Gossip, I wagered, would beat him at Punchestown. Tango was the reigning World Champion and his dressage was excellent. The likelihood of Gossip conquering this hero was as remote as a fish surviving on dry land. The idea, however, appealed greatly to my sense of the ridiculous.

To our astonishment Gossip did achieve the impossible on the dressage day at Punchestown when he beat the American pair by one point. We reckoned the leprechauns were definitely favouring the native-bred horse. No one could believe their eyes either when they watched Gossip's excellent performance or when they saw his score. For me the joke continued, and when I next saw Bruce, I found it irresistible to beam, 'So far, so good.'

How well I remember Punchestown in its early years: the days when the cross-country course was built of somewhat ungenerous timber, when not all the watches were synchronised, when I lay in the sun by a hedgerow for perhaps half an hour waiting for the starter to arrive so that we could start Phase A, albeit thirty minutes late.

Over the last few years a small band of hard-working people has taken a great deal of trouble to build up Punchestown to a highly respectable standard.

In 1981 the steeplechase course rode too long, the time impossible to obtain in the heavy ground. In true Irish style, the second 'half' was actually longer than the first. In 1982 nothing had changed except the going was much faster and it was common knowledge that it rode long. Unfortunately a complaint was lodged that the steeplechase was wrongly measured and this was forcefully driven through by one of the competitors. With only one hour remaining before the official start of the speed and endurance phase, the organisers altered the course.

As it turned out, the hastily renewed steeplechase track rode hopelessly short, so much so that I was already walking by the time we came through the finish.

Following Phase B, Gossip and I were trotting along the roads and tracks of Phase C at the same time as Botany Bay and David were going across country. We were able to watch them jumping beautifully over a few fences. They did not appear to be going particularly fast and therefore I was surprised to learn that they had completed Phase D within the time allowed.

As Gossip prepared to start the cross-country I heard over the loudspeakers that Bruce Davidson was having a second refusal on the course. Might Tango was obviously no longer on his old form and I began to regret having entered our wager. All Gossip had to do now, I felt, was go clear and he would be comfortably in the lead. Now fourteen years old, he had made sixteen appearances at three-day events. He had been second three times, on each occasion missing winning by the narrowest margin. I wondered if he might possibly be close to enjoying his first victory.

137

Village Gossip at Punchestown, 1982. He was distinctly dubious about this jump into water following his experience at Locko nine months earlier. (*M. Ansell*)

Gossip never goes anywhere slowly, and with the knowledge that Botany Bay, never renowned for speedy times, was within the limit, I saw no need to bustle unduly.

That was narrow vision on my part and definitely the last time I shall underestimate my husband's ability to ride the shortest, neatest course possible and come home with an excellent time.

Gossip was in the lead by the end of that day but with less than a show-jump in hand from Botany Bay, having earned himself six time faults. Only Botany Bay had no time faults and no others as few as Gossip.

Four of the British horses suffered bruised or cut heels, from,

Botany Bay and David jump an unusually fluent clear round. Punchestown, 1982. (*M. Ansell*)

we presumed, one stony patch on the course. Gossip was very sore on his heel, which became an angry red by the evening. Once again Joanna began her vigil with the ice and the kettle, alternating the temperature of the water in which Gossip's foot stood. Once again we witnessed how the good old-fashioned remedy of hot and cold can draw out bruising and by the morning, thanks to Joanna's conscientious and determined ministrations, Gossip was pain-free and completely sound.

That afternoon David produced the second of only two clear show-jumping rounds in the whole competition. Botany Bay's show-jumping talents are sparse; he had knocked four fences down

at Bicton three weeks earlier. They therefore both deserved the victory that Gossip, somewhat out of character, decided to give them when he booted one fence down with a front leg.

So ended yet another wonderful Punchestown, where the organisers' confessed main aim was that we should all enjoy ourselves. David won his first three-day event in the northern hemisphere and Gossip was second by 0.2 of a mark.

With all the horses languishing for a few weeks in summer grass up to their tummies, we departed to Australia. Once again I was destined to ride at Gawler. This time I was lent a Trakehner dressage stallion. Although I found riding him in dressage the hardest part, there being several different buttons in an area where I was used to only one, he went well if understandably immaturely across country. We had one refusal, relegating us to ninth place.

During this stay in Australia we learned for the first time that the International Equestrian Federation (FEI) had decreed that competitors could take part in commercial advertising. Previously competitors had only been allowed to do this if classified as professional which, in our sport, meant ineligibility for European, World and Olympic Championships. The definition of a non-professional is someone who is not paid to ride; however, any amount of his horses' expenses can be met by a commercial or private sponsor. We hoped this new rule would make our search for sponsorship easier. It did not, in the end, seem to make much difference. We continued to be met with negatives or unimaginative company policies that were nonetheless hard to argue. Many companies, it seemed, preferred to underwrite a competition, which would always be there on display and from which a winner would inevitably emerge. An individual, on the other hand, may have a fall, break a leg and not be there at all. What was worse, some felt there could be a possibility that their rider might not win, which would reflect unflatteringly on their product.

The autumn season of 1982 was destined to be an extremely busy one, particularly the month of September. If all went well,

---

Gossip fails to see the funny side. He knocked down a fence and was relegated to second place behind a stable-mate four years his junior. (*M. Ansell*)

141

ABOVE LEFT: Gig (left) and Alison about their duties. Mairangi is in the background in one of the three new stables that form part of David's yard in the old dairy. (*Stuart Newsham*) ABOVE RIGHT: Camilla at work. (*Stuart Newsham*) BELOW: Part of the tack-room wall displays various three-day event mementos, particularly stable-door name-plates. (*Stuart Newsham*)

ABOVE LEFT: Tomato is always the first into the horsebox if he senses an expedition is about to be made. (*Stuart Newsham*) ABOVE RIGHT: Alison takes care of top hat and tail coat. (*Stuart Newsham*)

---

the World Championships in Luhmühlen, Germany, were to take place the first weekend in September, Burghley the second, America the fourth, with Boekelo, Holland, following as the finale in mid-October. In our stables were eight Advanced horses, all of whom were aimed at one of these major internationals.

In June we divided our stable-yards before the autumn season started. David had his horses and his own head girl, Camilla Cholmeley, and number two, Alison Hicks, in the farm-yard fifty metres above the house-yard where mine were stabled. Jo was ostensibly my head girl aided by Gig Lees, but Jo knew exactly what was going on in every stable in both yards.

As a result of my initial trip to Australia back in 1979, Jill Rymill subsequently came to Appleshaw two years later as 'grook' (groom-cum-cook). She spent most of 1982 feeding the multitudes

143

of people that passed through our family home, as well as helping to look after the horses.

In addition to eight Advanced horses were a handful of youngsters that were eventing at Novice level. People wonder why my young horses do not perform polished dressage tests. They probably would if there was time to school them methodically and regularly. An event horse's daily training programme is generally infinitely more time-consuming and complex than that of either a show-jumper or a dressage horse. We reckon that to train properly, four horses each is ideal, five is feasible, but with six it is impossible to do sufficient justice to each, every day.

The first and last important one-day event before the World Championships was the National Championship at Locko. It was Regal Realm's first outing since Badminton and he confirmed his place in the British team by motoring effortlessly around the excellent course. It was the first event that year in which he pulled only politely.

Our ride at Badminton had been fast and on occasions he had thrown up his head so high that I found myself out of control. At home, watching repeatedly the video of his round there, David and I had decided to reverse the spring thought process and try him in a very short martingale. It had the desired effect and he became a little easier when his head was not allowed the full range of upward movement from the elastic-band which forms his neck.

At Locko I also experimented with a sawn-off whip. The normal length of a jumping whip is about twenty-eight inches; my new edition was only nineteen inches long. It seemed that each time I gathered up the reins after landing over a fence, Poncho would habitually retract his head and neck and then become frightened by the close proximity of my whip to his face. It had the effect of making him swerve away at increasing speed. A nineteen-inch

---

ABOVE: Regal Realm's show-jumping had become much calmer by Locko, 1982. Although he pulls very hard he has an extra-sensitive mouth as can be seen by the delicate contact I need to have over a fence. (*Kit Houghton*)

BELOW: Mairangi and David, Locko, 1982. A misjudgment in a double and Mairangi caught a pole between his legs and crashed. Fortunately both were all right. (*Stuart Newsham*)

144

whip is barely long enough to make contact with the horse's back-side should a reminder be necessary. I reckoned, however, it was worth the risk and should Poncho require its use I felt sure that, somehow, what little there was of it would find its target.

Poncho's show-jumping had improved greatly since the spring. As I write these words he has not yet knocked down a fence in competition.* By Locko he had become much more mature and rhythmic in his approach to each obstacle. He pulled himself up from fifth to second place with his clear show-jumping round. Both Jo and I independently reflected that George had also been second at Locko before he went on to win the European Championships at Burghley in 1977. Neither of us offered this thought to the other as we were both quite certain that Poncho was too inexperienced and not yet ready to start chasing individual titles. His dressage was not good enough for that, but his jumping had so far proved reliable and he should make an excellent team horse. If Beagle Bay and I had not been transformed into Pony Club pot-hunters at Locko, things may have been very different. Chasing the clock with all we had I rode like an imbecile and much too fast into the last fence. Beagle Bay missed his stride and lurched through the birch of the brush-fence. He did not fall but I fell off. Had that not happened and he had won the Championships, as both were short-listed, the selectors might have given me the choice of which horse to ride at Luhmühlen. With Regal Realm's dressage still fathoms below Continental standards, I would seriously have considered opting for Beagle Bay.

Poncho's flat-work had been improving a fraction that summer, until a week before Locko when he showed us the side of his temperament that he showed Merv all those years ago when Merv had first tried to shoe him. David Hunt rode him during a lesson for no longer than twenty minutes to bring him on a step further in his education. Whether it was the extra pressure he put on him, or the fact that David rides with a much firmer leg than me, I do not know, but the result was the same as when Merv walloped him with the shoeing rasp.

The next day when I schooled him he immediately tensed his

---

*I had barely put down my pen before Poncho made his first-ever error, at Crookham, the opening event of 1983. He tried to bounce a one-stride double and landed in the middle of the second element.

Beagle Bay and I jump the penultimate obstacle at Locko with the sort of gay abandon that brought me a deserved fall at the next and final fence. August, 1982. (*Kit Houghton*)

back, thereby suffocating most of his forward movement. He rejected the bit and stiffened into a hollow outline. My technique of riding dressage is unquestionably poor. When an awkward situation arises, particularly if it is near to a competition, I do not yet have enough confidence or certainty of direction in my flat-work skills to ride through the problems. I retract in much the same way as Poncho does.

The more I tried to rediscover our equilibrium, the more he declined to soften. Eventually there was nothing else to do except to return to the long and low outline we had worked at during the previous autumn. Even that took us a week to regain with any confidence. Four weeks later as we warmed up for our dressage test in the World Championships, I was still working him in the same manner.

The evening we returned from Locko and ten days before we were due to go to Germany, Helen Carr's little Australian horse, Champagne Charlie, produced a virus. Immediately he was isolated and the important three-day event prospects were stabled up in David's yard in the thin hope that being a bit further away from the sick horse might help avoid the bug. For a week we waited, taking temperatures daily, as everyone made a big effort to use the buckets of disinfectant placed in appropriate spots. Extraordinarily, all the horses escaped infection. A virus in a stable at any time is a much feared curse and particularly shortly before the World Championships. We were very, very lucky indeed that this one did not close down our activities for the remainder of the season.

During that week another Australian arrived at home, but only on a temporary basis. Emma D'Arcy came to help look after the horses whilst we were away competing for the greater part of September. She never left, and by the middle of 1983 she had

Emma, who joined us temporarily in September 1982 and stayed on to become David's head girl. (*Stuart Newsham*)

Gossip discovers the ultimate practical joke during his dressage test at Rotherfield Park One-Day Event, August, 1982. 'At X halt. Salute ...' (*Findlay Davidson*)

learnt the ropes and risen to manage David's yard, Camilla having departed earlier to be married.

Merv and Regal Reign and Andrew Hoy and Davey were in England preparing for Luhmühlen. David and Mairangi were asked to make up their team of three to represent Australia.

The British team comprised Ginny Holgate with Priceless, Rachel Bayliss with Mystic Minstrel, Regal Realm and myself and Richard Meade with Kilcashel. They were to run in that order in Luhmühlen. Diana Clapham and Windjammer, and Clarissa Strachan and her gallant fourteen-year-old Merry Sovereign, were the two British individual representatives.

Five days before we were due to leave for Hamburg we collected together for the second of two short terms of team training at Wylye, under the leadership of *chef d'équipe* Malcolm Wallace.

The second and final time in team training is an unwinding period. The day before it began, I rode three horses at the Rotherfield One-Day Event. Shannagh, improved beyond all recognition, was third in a hotly contested Open class in which he began to show some thoroughly exciting form. For the next four days of training at Wylye we would ride only three horses each day, we would eat and sleep at proper intervals for the right amount of time and one way and another we would become civilised human beings again. Only once or twice did I drive home to ride a few horses or to discuss and settle lengthy plans of what each horse was to do during our two weeks' absence. The time spent in team training is the necessary calm before the storm and I would be sorry to miss its full benefit.

In 1982 we had a team in which all six of us pulled together and enjoyed each other's company more than in any other team I can remember. We lived in a friendly, happy atmosphere in which thoughtfulness existed.

Each day we could have our own dressage trainer at Wylye if we wanted. Each day my jumping mentor of fourteen years was there to aid anyone who needed assistance with either grid exercises or course-jumping. Pat Burgess has helped me with every horse I have ever ridden, some of whom have had more problems than others. She has been repeatedly responsible for saving me from disaster when my weight begins to creep in front of my horse's centre of balance. This is a tiny fault and can happen so very easily, frequently with devastating effects on the horse's jump, particularly across country. If someone were to ask what was my greatest riding asset across country I would be bound to answer: sitting a fraction behind the horse's movement. With a bit of help from Jupiter, my first pony, who refused to jump unless I did that, it was Pat who drove into me the value of this concept.

During the week at Wylye we received wonderful news. John Burbidge, Shannagh's owner, lifted an immense load from David's and my shoulders. He indicated that he was nearly certain that his company, SR Direct Mail, would be able to take over our

Pat Burgess has helped me with every horse since Be Fair. (*David Green*)

The 1982 World Championship team was the happiest one I have been involved with during nine years of team membership. From left to right: Diana Clapham, Ginny Holgate, Richard Meade, Rachel Bayliss, Clarissa Strachan and myself. (*Kit Houghton*)

---

sponsorship when OCL's finished at the end of the year. It was more than provident that I had not severed the relationship with John Burbidge three months earlier, when, despairing of Shannagh's future, I had almost decided to return him to his owner.

Without mentioning it to each other, both David and I had become increasingly concerned with how much the results of the World Championships would affect our future. It was proving so difficult to attract sponsorship for ourselves that we feared failure in Luhmühlen might sound the finish of our international careers and the necessity to start life in Australia.

It was enormously relieving, therefore, to depart for the World Championships knowing that their outcome would not now be quite so crucial to our future.

At 6.30 a.m. on Friday, August 27th, travelling in a magnificent new horse-box lent to the team by its Lambourn manufacturers, Regal Realm and Jo, along with two other team horses and their grooms, set off in state for Harwich Docks. The other three horses and grooms enjoyed equal comfort in the horse-box belonging to Ginny Holgate's sponsors, British National Insurance. The remainder of us followed in two loaned Range-Rovers and a car. As we passed the turning to Appleshaw, David, chauffeuring the entire Australian entourage in one small horse-box loaned by the Devitt Equestrian Insurance Plan, joined the convoy.

The journey to Luhmühlen took thirty-four hours. Eighteen of these were spent on board the Harwich to Hamburg ferry and the remainder either in road travel or waiting the usual dreary hours for the paperwork and customs to be cleared at the ports.

Malcolm, his wife, Caroline, and I drove ahead of the convoy through Hamburg and on towards Lüneburg in order to prepare the stables.

Luhmühlen holds many memories for me, some of which have transported me nearly to Heaven and others which have engulfed me in sadness. On our first visit in 1975 Be Fair rendered himself an unexpected and undreamed-of European Champion. Gossip was second in the German Championships held there, two years later. In 1979 Killaire was in line for a medal in that country's second staging of the European Championships when he became inexplicably lame a few hours after he had finished the cross-country in third place. I cared nearly as deeply for that horse as I did for Be Fair. Just as his complete honesty was always tested to its utmost in a three-day event so were his limited abilities stretched to theirs. Never did his courage fail him. He was robbed of a diamond for his crown at Luhmühlen because the hard-packed sandy going had concussed his front feet. Killaire was declared a non-runner for the third day at the vets' inspection the morning after the cross-country. I was leading him out for a bite of grass

153

when this declaration was made. I have to admit that I found the only available cover, a meagre telegraph pole, two hundred yards from where the crowds stood craning to watch the inspection, and slumped down at its base in tears of sorrow for the incredible but injured horse that stood quietly grazing in front of me.

As we drove into the stable area, the heart of any international competition, I sighted that same meagre telegraph pole and, for a moment, I wondered whether or not I would be needing its minimal protection again.

We barely had time to climb out of our car before we were greeted with habitual friendliness by the director of the event, Dr Specht. We were shown which section of the three large barns of indoor stabling were for our use and we set about collecting heavy bales of peat from a nearby store to distribute in each stable as bedding.

No sooner had we completed this task than two huge horse-boxes with English number-plates rumbled onto the tarmac in front of the stable blocks.

The horses were unloaded and walked around the small nearby paddocks for half an hour before being introduced to their new homes. We left Poncho's bandages on for a while as we feared he might bang his legs on the walls of his box, which measured barely ten feet square.

All the horses were inspected briefly by the official vet. Horses cannot be eliminated from the competition at this inspection but if a horse appears distinctly unhealthy he can be isolated, thereby lessening any possible spread of disease. Any horse which does not trot up sound on arrival will be given a more thorough check at the official vetting which takes place the day before the dressage. Mairangi Bay's name went into the vet's notebook for just this reason. To our horror he trotted up very stiff behind and the stiffness increased over the following hour. We asked the British team vet, Peter Scott-Dunn, to look at him. Peter felt he had contracted cramp from the long journey despite the two statutory thirty-minute walks each horse had been given during their travelling. We stood him under a row of infra-red lamps that the German organisers had thoughtfully provided, while Alison and David hand-massaged his loins and back. Peter felt that no more should be done until we had allowed Mother Nature, in the shape of a good night's sleep, to take her course.

The next morning Mairangi must have wondered why we all looked so tense as we approached him with a halter. He was one hundred per cent sound when he was trotted along the tarmac.

Poncho settled in well. He revelled in the attention he was given by Joanna. She had no other horse on whom to lavish her attention, twenty-four hours a day. During his luxurious week in Germany Poncho risked eating his first Polo mint.

It is Luhmühlen tradition that our team is housed in the Josthof, a small rustic hotel which reflects the rural friendliness of its native Lower Saxony. In 1982 the warm-hearted proprietors gave me what they thought had been my lucky 1975 bedroom, the one in which I had slept when Be Fair had won the European Championships. My superstitions were not sure how to react on discovering that they had, in fact, mistakenly allotted me the bedroom next door to the lucky one.

David and I shared one night of our combined attack on the World Championships. Following this it became prudent to segregate. World Championship organisers are not accustomed to housing a husband and wife who are competing for different countries. The Australian team were in an hotel eight miles away. Whatever David's *chef d'équipe* may have said to him, we both felt vibes of discontent from the small Australian camp. Recognising the innate importance of team spirit we realised that we must go our separate ways for the week we spent in Germany. This did not mean that we were not constantly together when we were with the horses, walking the course or during the competition itself.

The day after our arrival there was little to do. The horses needed only a quiet walk in the morning. The Australian and British contingents were invited to Sunday lunch by a British Army brigadier in Hohne, thirty miles away. On the way there Malcolm registered his only failure of the whole trip when he mis-read his map and, amidst much amusement, caused us all to become totally lost and nearly an hour late.

Following an excellent lunch many of us left early to visit nearby Belsen. This infamous site is where hundreds of thousands of people, mostly Jews and political prisoners, were starved to death during the Second World War. It is now a tourist sight which ought to be witnessed. The jovial Sunday-lunch mood evaporated with alacrity before we had walked a hundred yards into the compound. Silently we wandered along paved tracks that divided four-foot-high rectangular mounds of varying sizes. By each mound was a small plaque indicating whether the number buried therein was in hundreds or thousands. This hideous relic of man's inhumanity to man stretched across a woodland clearing some half a mile square. Around the perimeter were trees, shrubs and grass. The prison area itself was sparse heathland, and only a few wilful sprigs of unflowering heather poked their way through the grey-brown sandy earth. Nothing seemed to want to live there. Death was pre-eminent in the stillness.

An hour later, as we walked out between the newly erected brick gate-turrets, we were struck by the sound of the birds, the green of the trees, the flowers in the bushes. We were, I think, struck by life itself.

It was an extraordinary experience and one for which I was quite unprepared. Over the past few weeks I had purposely led as superficial an existence as possible. If I allow myself to delve too deeply into my emotions shortly before a major competition it can sometimes cause me to lose control of my nerves.

Team spirit strengthened by the day, as we each deliberately tried to remember to make sure that our companions were all right. We watched with amusement as all twelve German competitors ran in procession on their personal daily fitness routine. (The host country is always allowed six extra individual entrants.) We sneaked into the stables of the Iron Curtain horses and found mostly small, wiry stallions from Russia, Bulgaria and Poland. We cast our eyes around the American boxes to see if we could pick up any tips on the latest technique of horse management, in order either to laugh at it or to adopt it, depending on our interpretation.

On occasions such as these many faces are familiar, but I find great difficulty in remembering names and nationalities to match them. It is wisest, therefore, to adopt a friendly attitude to all. Ignoring people is insulting and hurtful and quickly builds hostility in a sport which has an enviable lack of such. When I first began to compete in big three-day events I will never forget the gratitude

I felt towards 'The Greats' – Mary Gordon-Watson, Mark Phillips, Richard Meade and Richard Walker among others – who took the time and trouble to make me feel a part of the sport when I was as insignificant as my little cream horse-box for two. Dick Stillwell once advised me, 'Make as many friends as you can on the way up, because there is no time to do so on the way down.'

At eight o'clock on Wednesday morning, a line of seventeen Mercedes mini-buses left the stables. Each displayed the national flag of its passengers on the inside of the windscreen. One of the world's leading cross-country course designers, Wolfgang Feld, headed the procession in a covered jeep, on a guided tour of the speed and endurance phase.

The first section of roads and tracks started conveniently close to the stables. We drove across three and a half miles of flat farm-land, mostly on tracks or stubble, until we arrived at the start of the steeplechase. This was built in a figure of eight around the main showground area, some two miles from the stables. The occupants of all seventeen mini-buses then began to walk the con-fusing course that formed Phase B. It became immediately obvious that it would be very easy to lose the way and make a turn either too early or too late across the diagonal of the figure of eight.

The steeplechase fences themselves were typically Continental, not the stiff birch that we are used to in England. Some were over four feet high with soft wisps of greenery protruding from the top; others were three-foot high banks with six inches of spruce along the crest. The penultimate comprised eighteen-inch high white railings in front of a twelve-foot stretch of open water.

Once the seventy-odd competitors had rejoined their mini-buses the convoy proceeded down the six miles of the second phase of roads and tracks, whose terrain was similar to that of Phase A.

Forty-five minutes later the mini-buses assembled in the Box, the roped-off area where the horses are vetted, washed down and allowed their ten-minute break before the cross-country. A multi-national crowd filtered through the start flags and across the field towards the first fence of the 1982 World Championships, a sub-stantial and beautifully inviting man-made expanse of gorse hedge with the words 'WM Luhmühlen 1982' (WM – *Weltmeisterschaft*

– World Championships) picked out across its face in the purple heather of Lüneburg Heath.

The first viewing of the cross-country fences is possibly the most important. It is the first and last time that the rider will see the fences exactly as the horse will, unaware, as he will be, of what may be beyond. Our team waited at the start until the main stream of walkers had disappeared. I hung back a little from my team-mates as I felt very strongly that I wanted to be alone to absorb this first sighting lest I miss something through chatting.

At every three-day event I like to walk the cross-country course three times. On the second of the three walk-rounds I am happy either to be helped or help others. On the third and final course walk I always prefer to be alone to ensure my full concentration is beamed into each and every problem.

And problems there were on this course of nearly maximum distance – four and threequarter miles in all.

The course-builder's major concern in a World Championship is that through testing the best horse and rider, there is a serious danger of overfacing the worst. Wolfgang Feld, in his masterly design, had answered this problem in the only way possible. Nine of the thirty-two fences presented a multiple of alternative routes, most of them offering an easier but slower way through. Luhmühlen's other chief characteristic lay in its lack of drop fences. There were only three throughout the entire course and one of these was into water.

It is wise at any competition to know the line of approach and method of jumping every route available, but when in a team, it is vital. It is imperative that a team member can ride to orders. For this reason it is beneficial not to take too great a dislike to a certain path through a fence, lest it is deemed necessary by the *chef*, as the competition progresses, to ride it that way.

The most difficult fence came early in the course at number six. It was a water complex with two equally complicated alter-native routes. Five individual efforts of jumping were involved and fences seven and eight followed within a few yards.

Two days before the cross-country Malcolm held a team meeting for us to discuss the individual fences with one another. Richard, Ginny and Diana were an unprecedented one and a half hours late for this meeting. Instead of the usual two and a half to three

159

hours of walking time, this course was unexpectedly taking four hours to study on foot. There were just so many intricate alternatives to fathom and memorise.

The course seemed a true and fair test for a World Championship. It appeared to be a little less demanding than either Lexington or Fontainebleau, but there were plenty of places that would sort out the goats. Despite Regal Realm's comparative inexperience and the fact that we had only been together for a year, I was confident that he would not be overfaced. It still concerned me that he might try to refuse if he was not quite certain, particularly in the middle of fence six, where he was asked to jump up onto a bridge out of water and immediately spring over a wooden seat off the bridge and down into more water, six feet beneath. We had only just survived an extremely awkward passage through Badminton's lake five months earlier.

During the evening following our introduction to the cross-country, the first vets' inspection was held on the tarmac outside the stables. Every horse presented was passed except for one from Mexico.

Most of the remainder of that evening was spent taking part in an opening-ceremony parade. Each country's anthem was played by a brass band and speeches in German were delivered out of three different throats. Finally the band played the theme tune for the Championships, the stirring music from 'Chariots of Fire'.

On Thursday, 1st September 1982, the Championships began. The first two days were to be filled with dressage. David and Mairangi were due to do their test mid-morning on the second day. Coincidentally Regal Realm and I followed only seven horses behind them.

David Hunt flew out to Germany to give Mairangi and David some help with their dressage. In the space of half an hour on Thursday evening and threequarters of an hour before the test the two Davids had Mairangi performing as no one had ever seen him before. He produced a soft but sizzling display of an art that looks so easy when performed well. With a score of 45 they lay sixth best in the world at the end of the two days of dressage.

On the Tuesday of that week, Poncho had pulled a muscle somewhere behind the saddle area. I should have known better, but

160

Mairangi and David commence the best test of their lives to finish sixth best in the world after the dressage phase. World Championships, Luhmühlen, 1982. (*Hugo Czerny*)

obviously I had concentrated too sternly on his dressage in those last few days when there was only one horse for me to ride. He became very sore and started to hop behind on any small circle or corner. Our team vet's wife, Annie Scott-Dunn, treated him daily with Faradaism as he stood under the infra-red lamps. No more circles were turned or schooling performed until the day of his dressage test. Then, riding him towards a long and low novice outline, I warmed him up. He gave his stretched muscle a tweak shortly before we entered the main arena, just enough to remind me that he had a sore spot and to ride him without asking too much.

Regal Realm entered the main arena with stands packed on either side and began a circuit of the white dressage boards. We were only halfway round when his head came up and back towards my chin; he shortened his stride and stiffened his back. This was unexpected and not a little worrying. His calm temperament had

161

Regal Realm rises to the occasion. He stretches out his neck, softens his back and tries his hardest. Luhmühlen, 1982. (*Jim Meads*)

never produced the sudden arena-nerves that many of my horses have been unable to control. Believing he was worried by the sight of a decorative pile of rocks and bushes at the entry end of the dressage arena, we slowed to a walk. I dropped the reins and allowed him to walk around several times in front of the offending sight. The bell rang. We had to gather ourselves together and start our test within sixty seconds. Confident that there was nothing amongst the rocks to hurt him he relaxed again. He concentrated then on only one thing, doing the best possible dressage test within his limited capabilities. He scored 47.8 and lay sixteenth on the eve of the most important day of his life.

Later in the afternoon Jo clipped his already fine coat from under his stomach in order that he would sweat less the next day. Still with an intrinsic fear of noises, Poncho tensed his whole body at the sound and feel of the clippers. In his early days he proved nearly impossible to clip, but just as he had deemed it prudent to stop his relentless bucking so he eventually decided that he should give the clippers and their clattering the benefit of the doubt. Although he now behaves he holds himself taut until the noise of the blades has stopped. He may have settled and relaxed in the past few months but the acutely developed sensitivity that he had been born with never lessened.

Cross-country day dawned bright, sunny and a perfect temperature for the horses. Normally I like to conserve my energy on cross-country morning. This time, however, I took off in a mini-bus with Diana Clapham, who was still unsure about her approach line into fence six, the Euro-Pond. As we passed the scoreboard we noticed that one of the earliest competitors had already been eliminated on the steeplechase. The unfortunate New Zealander Ross Renwick and The Politician had fallen victim to the constant changes of direction and had made one of the changes too early.

Despite vehement protests from the army guards who were trying to keep spectators behind the crowd-barriers that lined the cross-country course, Diana and I managed to walk the route we both wanted to take into fence six. Suddenly a sharply blown whistle heralded the approach of the next competitor. We shot back under the ropes and waited for the action.

Fighting his gag bridle and showing little inclination to slow down, the long-striding Australian bay, Regal Reign, swept around the turn in front of us and faced up to the Euro-Pond. Merv approached the fence faster than I would have, but he knew his partner of seven years, and the big, scopey thoroughbred did not think twice as he flashed impressively through the combination. I remembered Merv's answer to Malcolm a few days earlier when asked whether he wished he still had Regal Realm: 'I think I kept the right one.' I began to see what he meant.

Shortly after this a small, extremely agitated Englishwoman, whom I had never seen before, gripped my arm. She urged me to ferry her across the course from one set of ropes to the other. It transpired that she was a runner for the British team and a guard was refusing to allow her to cross the course in order that she could return to her post.

There were over fifty British helpers, drawn from neighbouring army regiments and from the large number of supporters who had come to Germany especially to cheer their home team.

163

Different people were directed to various fences for intervals of two hours or longer. Messengers were attached to each fence and they ran, sometimes two or three miles, back to the start with news about how the course was riding.

Head of the selection committee, Chris Collins, was at work in the Box acting as computer to all the information received. He and Malcolm would discuss the outcome and agree on what advice the latter should give to the next British rider who came into the Box.

My mother supports both sides of the world. (*Lady Anne Whiteley*)

Annie Scott-Dunn during an unserious moment in the Box. She took on the task of keeping abreast of scores and team positionings throughout the entire day. (*Lady Anne Whiteley*)

Early in the afternoon I disappeared into the *Damen* next to the stables. There I sat for a full twenty minutes, head in hands, eyes tightly closed. Filtering through my mind were the images of every yard and each fence of the steeplechase and cross-country courses that in under two hours Regal Realm and I hoped to encounter.

I materialised in time to give David a leg up onto Mairangi and to wish him the best of everything as he started on the first phase. Half an hour later Poncho and I trotted strongly through the same start, his ears familiarly close to my mouth, his narrow little body wriggling from side to side underneath me until we both united into a more balanced trot.

We did not lose our way round the steeplechase, and although

David and Mairangi, six fences from home, come down the steps in balance and security. (*Kit Houghton*)

Poncho was thoroughly suspicious of the strange-looking fences and therefore jumped most of them much too high, he was fifteen seconds within the five-minute time limit.

After six further miles of sandy forest tracks, stubble fields and country road verges, we trotted through the finish flag of Phase C. Almost immediately I spotted David on his feet on the far side of the Box. He had finished his round on Mairangi; I could not wait to hear how they had fared. I signalled to him: thumbs up, or thumbs down? He responded with a thumbs down. I had to wait patiently until the vet had finished checking Poncho before I could discover what had gone wrong.

Mairangi had given David a superb ride but at the half-way

point they had taken the quicker route over a stone-faced Irish bank. Mairangi had failed to appreciate that it was a bank and not a wall and consequently had not straightened his legs in time. He landed on folded knees on the top of the bank and rolled gently over. It lost everything for them, but it may have saved it for us. Although I had not liked that route, it was much shorter and of the other two riders who had attempted it, both had been successful. One of those two was Regal Reign who finished the course with only 5.2 time penalties. Until learning of Mairangi's fall, I may well have decided, at the last minute, to take that route.

Malcolm sat me down on a small canvas chair in the British section of the Box. My orders were simple. Rachel and Mystic Minstrel had suffered a refusal at the fourth and most difficult part of fence six, putting the German and American teams ahead of the British. Would Regal Realm, therefore, please come home with a clear round and no time penalties? It was not asking the impossible. Over two-thirds of the seventy-seven competitors had completed their cross-country rounds, and one Pole and one American were clear and within the time limit.

Malcolm was keen that I should take the quickest route over the walled bank where Mairangi had fallen. My instincts told me from the first sighting that the quick route held a lower margin for error than balanced the risk. Malcolm sensed my unease. Quickly he weighed the odds and changed tactics: 'Well, he's a very fast horse. If you'd be happier taking the longer route, I should do that.'

Suitably refreshed, and with the fronts of his legs greased with Vaseline to help him slide out of difficulty over a fence, Regal Realm and I walked quietly towards the start of the crucial cross-country phase of the 1982 World Championships.

Regal Realm does not play havoc in the starting box. For one so courageous and keen it is extraordinary that he has such a calm disposition. Despite over a decade of practice, I still have a fight to quell paralysing thoughts of how much depends on the next thirteen minutes; of the awful mistakes I might make and how they might hurt my horse. There is always a quiet voice within asking 'Why, why do I do it?'

'Three, two, one. Go!' was translated into three short bleeps and one longer note on an electrical starter. Poncho shot out of

167

the small pen and pelted towards the first fence. His head came up and back as his neck twisted round almost back to front. He was always difficult to ride early on in the course, before he settled. He crossed his legs on a tight turn that he was not expecting in the woods and very nearly came down. That incident proved helpful if unnerving. Thereafter he listened a little more to my requests to slow down.

A huge roar from an appreciative crowd, ten deep around fence six, greeted Poncho as he sprang bravely off the bridge and back down into the water. For an instant he hesitated as he alighted on the bridge. He used that fraction of time to sum up the situation, but such a moment could easily have turned into a refusal.

Even my athletic little strip of India rubber needed the extra propulsion supplied by my mini-whip as he faced up to fence eight, and his seventh leap in the space of a hundred yards. It was the part of the course that tested most searchingly the abilities of horse and rider. There still remained over threequarters of the course in front of us.

Poncho surged ahead. As he sprang over the first part of some of the more complex combinations I could feel for a split second his amazement at what he saw in front of him. Undaunted he sped on. It was exhilarating to feel the panache with which he tackled one imposing question after another.

By the last quarter of the course he was becoming very strong and difficult to ride. I knew that the final few obstacles were akin to the difficult combination fences we had encountered early in the course. In between fences I had allowed him to go as fast as he wanted in order to preserve his peace of mind and reserve my own strength for when I must ask him to come back to me and slow down, no matter what, in front of those final obstacles.

He threw up his head even higher as he resisted my attempts to reduce speed. Possibly he barely saw several elements of the penultimate fence, which consisted of a multiple of fences involving water again. He galloped across the finish line and kept going as fast as he could despite my assurance that it was no longer necessary. Only one other horse I had ridden possessed this extraordinary, apparently tireless capacity to gallop and jump – Village Gossip. Where others may struggle through the finish, those two horses would still be in full chorus.

ABOVE: We land safely in the water at the final element of the penultimate fence. (*Kit Houghton*)

PRECEDING PAGE: Regal Realm at the steps, judging his descent with interest. (*Jim Meads*)

It was probably not until that moment that the pressure of riding for my country really asserted itself. A swell of relief filled me. That brilliant little upside-down Australian cattle pony had given his new rider all that was needed.

Poncho was washed down and led back to the stables by a thankful Joanna whose paling cheeks had returned to a more healthy colour.

I waited for Richard Meade and Kilcashel to return from Phase C in case Richard wanted to seek any advice before setting out on the cross-country. Meanwhile I discovered how fantastically well Britain's two individual riders had done. Both Clarissa's Merry Sovereign and Diana's Windjammer had gone clear with only 8.4 and 6 time penalties respectively.

Richard's orders were similar to mine: for the team to have a chance he must go clear and within the time. With the accuracy of timing that must come after nearly twenty years of top-class competition, Richard and Kilcashel produced what was required.

Forty-one horses had gone clear during the day but only five were within the time limit. Kilcashel's and Regal Realm's faultless journeys, along with Priceless's path-finding venture of a clear round with 8.8 penalties, squeezed Britain into the slimmest of leads with a total of 162.40 penalties. The Americans trailed by a mere 1.4 points and Germany were a further 0.8 behind them.

Never before in a World Championship had the scores been so absurdly close at this stage.

To my amazement Regal Realm lay second individually, 5.8 points behind Germany's Helmut Rethemeier on Santiago. In third place was the American, Kim Walnes, on The Gray Goose. The reigning dual World Champion, Bruce Davidson, riding J.J Babu, the horse that had won him second place at Badminton in the spring, was clear but surprisingly slow across country, finishing in twenty-first place.

It was not until the day's excitement had finished that David and I learned of the tragedy that had occurred earlier. No horses had been hurt but the Swiss rider, Ernst Baumann, had been killed. He was riding the Swiss reserve horse borrowed from a team-mate, as his own was found to be lame on arrival. He had succeeded in reaching the last water fence, the Duck Pond, but the massive fifteen-year-old chestnut stallion had somersaulted over the fourth

171

element onto the ejected body of his rider. The fall was no worse than those seen regularly in many horse sports, but this one proved instantly fatal.

The competitors' party that night was cancelled. No one felt like rejoicing when thinking of the young wife and family Ernst had left behind.

At 9.30 p.m. all the British horses trotted out for a private vetting. None were so free and springy in their stride as my little brown stock horse with the lucky white sock. But then, unlike the others, he was brought up in the outback on iron-hard ground.

Regal Reign had cut a hind pastern and so the Bennetts were up most of the night treating his leg. When we went into the Australian tack-room that evening, we tripped over the two sleeping bodies of Merv and Ann huddled together under a horse blanket. They were trying to snatch some rest in between cold compresses. We left them in peace and tip-toed out again.

The following day someone expressed surprise when I replied that I had slept very soundly. 'I could not have slept if I was in your position.' It never struck me with any force that there was anything to be extra nervous about. In my mind I thought that Santiago, being a graded show-jumper, would make no mistakes in the show-jumping and my confidence that Poncho would do the same was high. I looked upon the show-jumping as a dicey and nerve-racking challenge for our team, however, with only 2.2 points in hand over both Americans and Germans. The individual gold medal was a long way from my mind – as it had been strangely enough, when lying second on George to another German, Karl Schultz, at the European Championships at Burghley in 1977.

Not long after the final official vetting on Sunday morning the teams were allowed to walk the show-jumping course. It was the toughest I have seen at a three-day event. The fences were comparatively big and very well built, and some of the related distances between them were awkward. It was a long, twisty course involving twelve obstacles, two of which were trebles. Unobtrusively Richard ensured that all the British riders were happy and had not missed any of the less obvious problems the course presented.

Before the show-jumping commenced the competitors rode into the arena and stood in a long row, side by side, across its centre.

For nearly five minutes a colourful tribute in German was paid to Ernst Baumann. At its close the Swiss national anthem was played as their flag was lowered to half-mast. It was a brief but extremely moving ceremony, throughout which the horses sensed the mood of the occasion and remained very still. Three hours later many of those same horses could barely contain themselves in a similar line-up for the prize-giving. Here, during this moment of mourning, was more proof of the extra-sensory perception that I have always believed horses possess and have strongly developed. It is a dimension of their senses which responds instantly to the vibrations of the human mood encircling them.

Later that afternoon I was particularly proud to be British. The show-jumping proved to be every bit as demanding as it looked. Poles were hitting the ground with alarming regularity. Each time a British rider jumped, there was a coolness and a decisive style which withstood the enormous pressures attendant, and the team recorded only two fences down out of six rounds. Pat Burgess' influence on the victorious World Championship team was there for all to see. The American team, on the other hand, suffered a less satisfying outcome with nine fences down.

Regal Realm was not as easy to show-jump as normal. His cross-country round, only twenty-four hours earlier, had probably rendered him a little less elastic. Even so, I only had to growl once down his ear as his front legs came too close to the edge of a pole. The last fence was a big parallel, only a few strides after the open water. Many horses had hit the parallel because they were still too flat and fast after spreading themselves across twelve feet of water. As Poncho landed over the penultimate fence, I pulled him back to try and bunch him up before the last. For two strides he stuck his head in the air and fought. The parallel was only a few yards away and we were on completely the wrong stride. There was no option but to give him his head and kick for a long stride and a huge stand-off. Ethically it was incorrect but it was instinctive and it worked. A thunderous applause from thousands of mostly Continental spectators greeted Regal Realm as he landed and galloped away. He would only stop when he came face to face with the crowd at the arena edge.

Before 1983, team championship events did not run the show-jumping in reverse order of merit but in programme order instead.

173

Helmut Rethemeier happened to be drawn in the programme only three horses after us.

Giving Poncho another grateful hug after I had weighed in, and clutching my small, twenty-year-old lucky teddy, I ran back to the arena entrance to watch Santiago's round. Only then did the pincers catch hold of my stomach and make me realise that there was a chance that Regal Realm could become World Champion.

I have always felt that the wrong way to win or lose a three-day event is in the show-jumping phase. The cross-country day is what it is all about. However, I have won and lost in both ways. If fortune should happen to favour me this time, I would not complain.

Helmut could afford one fence down and still maintain his lead. He rattled several rails early in the course but none fell to the ground. My tension lessened, he was over the most difficult fences and he had survived; with that sort of luck he would be all right.

His luck ran out. In an attempt to make his horse jump more carefully he rode him slower and tighter, a feeling I know so well. The first element of the treble came down, and, incredibly, so did the second.

That was it. Regal Realm had become the new Champion of the World, a title he would own for a further four years. Crinkling up in a daze Teddy and I dropped to the ground.

Half an hour later Kilcashel made only one mistake. The British team therefore maintained its lead.

After two individual European Championships and four Badmintons, I honestly thought that I must have exhausted my quota of wins and that never again would I hit the big-time. I found it genuinely hard to believe that it had happened; and there was nothing superstitious about it. Seven is my lucky number, we were no longer in the seventies and Poncho's number during the competition had been fifty-eight. He was the only horse in the world to finish the Championships adding nothing further to his dressage penalties.

Despite seeing his gold medal fade to silver, Helmut Rethemeier was the model of a good sportsman. His warmth and good humour were unforgettable. Regal Realm stands bedecked as Champion. (*Hugo Czerny*)

ABOVE: The victory wreath was not made for a small stock horse. To prevent Regal Realm from hooking his front legs through the oak leaves I had to hitch the garland over my arm, control Regal Realm and thank him all at the same time. (*Jim Meads*)

OPPOSITE ABOVE: The winning team. Richard, Ginny, Rachel and myself lap the arena at speed. (*Jim Meads*)

OPPOSITE BELOW: Terry Walsh from OCL witnessed an occasion that would never have happened without five years of their life-giving sponsorship. (*Kit Houghton*)

Standing alone on the rostrum, watching the Union Jack rise to the top of the highest flag-pole as our National Anthem ricocheted around the stands, something crossed my mind. In 1975 I had been standing in the same place in precisely the same arena after the European Championships had been won by Be Fair. That was exactly seven years ago.

EPILOGUE

Dear Lucinda —

I have a strong feeling that Regal Realm
is going to win Badminton this year.
Very, very good luck for the event.
With best wishes from one
of many supporters.

This letter arrived at the beginning of Badminton week in 1983. Although I believed it was merely the wishful-thinking of a kind fan, I told no one.

By the end of the week Regal Realm had won the world's most prestigious three-day event, displaying talents that placed him in a realm of his own. He was in reality the horse that I did not believe could exist.

1982 World Championship Results

INDIVIDUAL PLACINGS

PLACE	NO.	RIDER	HORSE	DRESSAGE	SPEED AND ENDURANCE	SHOW-JUMPING	Points
1	58	Lucinda Green (GBR)	Regal Realm	47·80	0·00	0·00	47·80
2	62	Helmut Rethemeier (GER)	Santiago	41·20	0·80	10·00	52·00
3	67	Kim Walnes (USA)	The Gray Goose	39·40	8·40	5·00	52·80
4	46	Rüdiger Schwarz (GER)	Power Game	41·40	14·40	0·00	55·80
5	73	Richard Meade (GBR)	Kilcashel	54·20	0·00	5·00	59·20
6	36	Clarissa Strachan (GBR)	Merry Sovereign	51·40	8·40	0·00	59·80
7	18	Virginia Holgate (GBR)	Priceless	51·60	8·80	0·00	60·40
8	16	Peter F. Green (USA)	Branch Water	52·60	0·80	10·00	63·40
9	27	Andrew Hoy (AUS)	Davey	57·60	6·00	0·00	63·60
10	42	Diana Clapham (GBR)	Windjammer	53·60	6·00	5·00	64·60
11	59	Thierry Lacour (FRA)	Hymen de la Cour	45·40	19·60	0·00	65·00
12	20	Patrick Marquebielle (FRA)	Flamenco III	53·00	8·40	5·00	66·40
13	24	Herbert Blöcker (GER)	Ladad	51·20	15·60	0·00	66·80
13	70	Bruce Davidson (USA)	J. J. Babu	45·20	21·60	0·00	66·80
15	32	Sven Ingvarsson (SWE)	Doledo	59·20	1·60	6·50	67·30
16	10	Jessica Harrington (IRL)	Amoy	61·40	6·00	0·00	67·40
17	33	Nancy Bliss (USA)	Cobblestone	47·40	6·40	15·00	68·80
18	38	Dieter Hesselbach (GER)	Royal Blue	61·40	4·00	5·00	70·40
19	1	Dietmar Hogrefe (GER)	Foliant 6	64·40	6·40	0·00	70·80
20	68	Boris Gortchakov (URS)	Netchiotnyi	55·00	11·60	5·00	71·60
21	11	Torrance Watkins Fleischmann (USA)	Southern Comfort	47·40	14·80	10·00	72·20
22	41	Rachel Bayliss (GBR)	Mystic Minstrel	35·80	36·80	0·00	72·60
23	35	Nils Haagensen (DEN)	Fair Lady	48·00	20·80	5·75	74·55
24	13	Bettina Overesch (GER)	Peace Time	57·80	20·40	0·00	78·20
25	2	Karen Stives (USA)	The Saint	60·20	13·20	5·00	78·40
25	43	Paul Loiseau (FRA)	Elding Bleu	50·20	13·20	15·00	78·40
27	44	Jan Lipczynski (POL)	Elektron	59·60	0·00	20·00	79·60
28	61	Simon de Jonge (HOL)	Miracle	50·40	14·80	15·00	80·20
29	75	Jacek Bobik (POL)	Koper	55·60	21·60	5·00	82·20
30	22	Gerard Sinnott (IRL)	The Prop	62·40	12·00	10·00	84·40
31	54	J. Michael Plumb (USA)	Blue Stone	52·40	32·80	0·00	85·20
32	53	Christian Persson (SWE)	Joel	55·40	24·80	6·50	86·70

33	6	Merv Bennett (AUS)	Regal Reign	74·40	5·20	8·00	87
34	28	Karl Siemens-Fischer (GER)	Kim	52·80	19·20	20·00	92
35	57	Kelly Plitz (CAN)	Dialadream	63·80	22·80	10·00	96
36	40	Nick Holmes-Smith (CAN)	Sinnerman	71·40	18·80	10·00	100
37	14	Alexandre Blinov (URS)	Zheti	55·40	41·60	5·00	102
38	49	Marina Sciocchetti (ITA)	Master Hunt	57·60	30·40	15·00	103
39	77	Mary Hamilton (NZL)	Ben Arthur	50·40	38·80	15·25	104
40	3	Pascal Morvillers (FRA)	Gulliver B	49·00	47·20	10·00	106
41	60	Krzysztof Rafalak (POL)	Dajak	45·00	64·80	0·00	109
42	31	Neil Ishoy (CAN)	L'Esprit	66·80	38·40	25·00	130
43	51	David Green (AUS)	Mairangi Bay	45·00	76·40	10·00	131
44	71	Robin Hahn (CAN)	Strathallan	75·20	46·40	11·25	132
45	76	Anchela Rohof (HOL)	Resolution Bay	45·80	79·20	17·25	142
46	65	Jan Jönsson (SWE)	Lyrik	50·00	77·20	16·75	143
47	72	Juliet Bishop (CAN)	Jones	62·20	70·00	15·00	147
48	8	Jean Teulere (FRA)	En Douce II	60·40	89·20	5·00	154
49	23	Miroslaw Szlapka (POL)	Len	53·00	120·00	0·00	173
50	37	Thomas Rüder (GER)	Maniok	47·40	137·20	0·00	184
51	15	Plamen Kirov (BUL)	Mentor II	69·80	105·60	10·25	185
52	5	Dino Constantini (ITA)	Demon Prince	65·20	116·00	6·00	187
53	12	Artur Bober (POL)	Czubczyk	75·40	120·80	0·00	196
54	17	Robert Robertson (CAN)	Jack The Lad	65·60	116·40	15·00	197
55	21	Martin Plewa (GER)	Little Lion	40·00	166·40	0·00	206
56	25	Jose-Luis Luna (MEX)	Quelite	76·80	145·20	6·50	228
57	55	Alexandre Zavistovski (URS)	Diamed	57·00	171·20	10·75	238
	34	Sergei Rogozhin (URS)	Referendum	53·80	32·00	WITHDR	
	29	Hansueli Schmutz (SUI)	Oran	46·20	40·40	WITHDR	
	26	Anna Casagrande (ITA)	Daleye	64·40	103·60	WITHDR	
	30	Friedrich Otto (GER)	Chicoa	55·40	128·40	WITHDR	
	50	Bernd Neumann (GER)	Banana	47·80	WITHDR		
	64	Sepp Burger (SUI)	Mr. Ickford	65·80	WITHDR		
	19	David Barcena (MEX)	Centauro	82·40	WITHDR		
	45	Wout-Jan v. d. Schans (HOL)	Harrock Hill	64·00	WITHDR		
	63	Jose Luis Perez (MEX)	Ayatollah	59·40	WITHDR		
	52	Sepp Räber (SUI)	Benno II	60·60	WITHDR		
	39	Djenko Sabev (BUL)	Afekt	59·20	WITHDR		
	48	Miroslaw Ślusarczyk (POL)	Asesor	53·40	42·00	ELIM	
	69	Tzvetan Dontchev (BUL)	Medison	53·80	ELIM		
	4	Salvador Suarez (MEX)	Bombona	67·20	ELIM		
	47	Roberto Redon (MEX)	Cristero	57·20	ELIM		
	66	Yury Salnikov (URS)	Akoprin	77·60	ELIM		
	74	Joel Pons (FRA)	Ensorceleuse	50·40	ELIM		
	7	Ross Renwick (NZL)	The Politician	55·60	ELIM		
	56	Dimo Kristov (BUL)	Maket	57·20	ELIM		

TEAM CHAMPIONSHIP

1. *Great Britain*

Lucinda Green	Regal Realm	47·80
Richard Meade	Kilcashel	59·20
Virginia Holgate	Priceless	60·40
Rachel Bayliss	Mystic Minstrel	(72·60)
		167·40

2. *Germany*

Helmut Rethemeier	Santiago	52·00
Rüdiger Schwarz	Power Game	55·80
Herbert Blöcker	Ladad	66·80
		174·60

3. *USA*

Kim Walnes	The Gray Goose	52·80
Nancy Bliss	Cobblestone	68·80
Torrance Watkins Fleischmann	Southern Comfort	72·20
		193·80

4. *France*

Thierry Lacour	Hymen de la Cour	65·00
Patrick Marquebielle	Flamenco III	66·40
Paul Loiseau	Elding Bleu	78·40
		209·80

5. *Poland*

Jan Lipczynski	Elektron	79·60
Jacek Bobik	Koper	82·20
Krzysztof Rafalak	Dajak	109·80
		271·60

6. *Australia*

Andrew Hoy	Davey	63·60
Merv Bennett	Regal Reign	87·60
David Green	Mairangi Bay	131·40
		282·60

7. *Sweden*   297·95
8. *Canada*   344·00
9. *USSR*   412·55

181

Interval Training

Many people have asked me to write about interval training but it is not a subject which can be written down comprehensively. Even attempting to put it on paper may be unwise. Horses are not machines, and although it is perfectly possible to give a breakdown of how a tractor can be made to work the same does not apply to making a horse fit. A little knowledge is a dangerous thing, but I dare not give more than an outline of the basic principle:

Following the initial six weeks of road work, schooling and the general beginnings of toning and hardening up, the programme can commence. The objective is to enable a horse to reach his peak of fitness with the minimum amount of wear and tear. Accordingly training sessions, or work-outs, take place once every three or four days, gradually increasing the amount of canter work at each session. Apparently it takes between three and four days for a horse to fully recover from a work-out. To work a horse any sooner is to work a tired limb and invite injury; to work him later will benefit the horse correspondingly less as his muscles are beginning to slacken. If a horse is becoming too fit too soon, spacing the work-outs at five-, six- or even seven-day intervals will effectively slow up his progress.

The length of each of the three canters involved in each work-out and of the two intervening periods of relaxation and walking should be calculated to produce a horse almost fully recovered during the first break and half to threequarters recovered during the second. If he is asked to work again just before he has recovered he will thereby increasingly expand his heart and lung capacity thus building up his fitness in relation. This is a more logical approach than conventional fitness-training programmes which often involve pounding on in canter for twenty minutes or more at a time.

In 1974 when Bruce Davidson first introduced me to the system I worked from a pattern. Basically it began with three sessions of three-minute canters at 400 metres a minute interspersed with two three-minute breaks – 3 (3) 3 (3) 3 – and it built up over intervals of four days to three ten-minute canters at 400 metres a minute with two three-minute breaks between each – 10 (3) 10 (3) 10. It was only during the last three or four work-outs that any fast work was incorporated.

It is speed that kills. Galloping breaks down a horse quicker than any other work. During the last three or four work-outs of any training programme, four to five furlongs at a threequarter-speed gallop is about as much as I do.

Over the years I have come to appreciate how impossible it is to write a formula for fitness because every horse is different and requires slightly different work. It soon became evident that three lots of ten-minute canters involved too much hard work for my particular horses. The right amount depends on the type of horse, its temperament and the terrain being used. Flat terrain will require longer slow cantering than will hilly terrain. Hilly terrain is ideal for cold-blooded horses (e.g. Killaire, Badminton 1979). In this case the canters can be reduced to a total of maybe only seventeen or eighteen minutes.

These may be broken up into only two lots with accelerations uphill to keep the horse's incentive and interest. Fast work up not too steep an incline produces far less strain on the legs than it does when carried out on the flat. Also, less distance needs to be covered when galloping uphill. However, when canter work is carried out on hills, descents should be gradual and at an angle to lessen any jarring on the front legs. When the going is very hard it is advisable to canter uphill or on the flat only.

The feeling required when developing a horse's fitness with slow work is the following: he must be pumping up against your hand and flexing his muscles every stride, not lolloping along. (Preferably not behaving like Gossip and fighting for freedom every stride, either.)

In preparation for Badminton 1979, Killaire's interval training

183

programme began at the end of February. Given below are details of the last seven weeks leading up to Badminton.

MARCH

Tues 6th	5 (3) 5 (3) 5 – on the flat, at 400 m/min (i.e. 1 mile per 4 mins)
Sat 10th	6 (3) 6 (3) 6 – on the flat, at 400 m/min
Tues 13th	6 (3) 6 (3) 6 – on the flat, at 400 m/min
Sat 17th	7 (3) 6 (3) 7 – on the flat, at 400 m/min
Tues 20th	7 (3) 7 (3) 7 – on the flat, slightly faster canter: 425–450 m/min
Sat 24th	8 (3) 6 (3) 8 – on the flat, slightly faster canter: 425–450 m/min
Tues 27th	7 (3) 8 – on hills, including three spurts uphill
Sat 31st	Rushall One-Day Event

APRIL

Fri 6th	8 (2½) 7½ – on hills, including three spurts uphill
Wed 11th	9 (3) 8 – on hills, including four spurts uphill
Mon 16th	7 (2½) plus ¾ mile gallop – on the flat
Thurs 19th	Cantered up a hill
Fri 20th	Pipe-opener up a hill
Sat 21st	Cross-country day, Badminton

NB: The intervening days are taken up with mostly walking and/or schooling. The day after each work-out should always be devoted either to a long walk or to resting.

Some horses will respond better to a programme wherein the number of minutes they canter in any one bout never exceeds six, but instead the speed is gradually increased. A useful programme can be worked out whereby the last minute of the second and third canters can be increased to 500 metres per minute and 600 metres per minute respectively, starting approximately eight work-outs before the three-day event. This routine can be continued until the speed of the final minute of each of the last two canters has increased to 550 metres per minute and 650 metres per minute respectively.

Vital Statistics

BE FAIR
Owned by the author
Born 1963
Bred in Gloucestershire by Miss Joan Rymer
16.2 h.h. chestnut gelding
By FAIR AND SQUARE (three-day event horse)
Ex HAPPY REUNION (classically bred mare; believed raced and
    hunted)
Member of gold medal team, Junior European Championships,
    Wesel, 1971; age 8 years
Won Badminton 1973; age 10 years
Won European Championship (Luhmühlen) 1975; age 12 years
Represented Great Britain at Montreal Olympics 1976; age 13 years

WIDE AWAKE
Owned by Mrs V. Phillips
Born 1966
Bred in Oxfordshire by Mr and Mrs Charles Cope
16.1 h.h. bay gelding
By HEREWARD THE WAKE (thoroughbred sire)
Ex SERENADE (three-day event mare)
Won Dutch International (Boekelo) 1975; age 9 years
Won Badminton 1976; age 10 years

GEORGE
Owned and bred in Yorkshire by Mrs H. Straker
Born in 1965
16.2 h.h. bay gelding
By ST GEORG (thoroughbred sire sold to Germany)
Ex WINNIFRITH (point-to-point and hunter mare)

Won Badminton 1977; age 12 years
Won European Championship (Burghley) 1977; age 12 years

KILLAIRE
Owned by Mr C. A. Cyzer
Born 1968
Bred in Northern Ireland
16.3 h.h. bay gelding
By CARNATIC (thoroughbred sire sold to Ireland)
Dam unknown
Second at Burghley 1976; age 8 years
Third at Badminton 1977; age 9 years
Third at Ledyard (USA) 1977; age 9 years
Won Badminton 1979; age 11 years
Second at Badminton 1980; age 12 years

VILLAGE GOSSIP
Owned by Mr David Kingsley
Born 1968 in Southern Ireland
16 h.h. dark brown gelding
By ARDFERT (thoroughbred sire)
Ex JUT GOLD (thoroughbred mare)
Second at Luhmühlen 1977; age 9 years
Second at Dutch International (Boekelo) 1977; age 9 years
Second at Badminton 1978; age 10 years
Seventh at Alternative Olympics (Fontainebleau) 1980; age
    12 years
Second at Irish International (Punchestown) 1982; age 14 years
Second at US Championships (Chesterlands) 1982; age 14 years

BEAGLE BAY
Owned by Mr David Kingsley and the author
Born 1970 in Shropshire
16.1 h.h. grey gelding
By PANNIER (thoroughbred sire)
Ex SOMETIMES (Grade B show-jumper)
Third Wylye Three-Day Event 1979; age 9 years
Won Burghley 1981; age 11 years

REGAL REALM
Owned by the author
Born November 1971 in Australia
16 h.h. brown gelding
By TAUNTON (thoroughbred sire)
Ex station-bred thoroughbred
Second Dutch International (Boekelo) 1981; age 9 years
Won World Championships (Luhmühlen) 1982; age 10 years
Won Badminton 1983; age 11 years

And one was there, a stripling on a small and weedy beast;
  He was something like a racehorse undersized,
With a touch of Timor pony – three parts thoroughbred at least –
  And such as are by mountain horsemen prized.
He was hard and tough and wiry – just the sort that won't say die –
  There was courage in his quick impatient tread;
And he bore the badge of gameness in his bright and fiery eye,
  And the proud and lofty carriage of his head.

But still so slight and weedy, one would doubt his power to stay,
  And the old man said, 'That horse will never do
For a long and tiring gallop – lad, you'd better stop away,
  Those hills are far too rough for such as you.'
So he waited, sad and wistful – only Clancy stood his friend –
  'I think we ought to let him come,' he said;
'I warrant he'll be with us when he's wanted at the end.'

From *A Man from Snowy River*
by Banjo Patterson, 1895